THE PROFESSIONAL JOB SEARCH PROGRAM

BOOKS BY BURTON E. LIPMAN

The Professional Job Search Program

How to Become a Vice President in Two Weeks (More or Less)

How to Control and Reduce Inventory

Successful Cost Reduction and Control

THE PROFESSIONAL JOB SEARCH PROGRAM

How to Market Yourself

BURTON E. LIPMAN

JOHN WILEY & SONS

New York Chichester Brisbane Toronto Singapore

Library of Congress Cataloging in Publication Data:

Lipman, Burton E., 1931–
   The professional job search program.

   Includes index.
   1. Job hunting.   2. Professions.   I. Title.
HF5382.7.L56   1983   650.1′4   82-25089
ISBN 0-471-89159-2 (cloth)
ISBN 0-471-82058-X (paper)

Printed in the United States of America

10 9 8 7 6 5 4

To all my friends, business associates, and supporters, a thank you for finally forcing me to set down on paper all of these techniques, so that others may share in their success.

To my wife, a vote of appreciation for putting up with the author before, during, and after this project.

To my entire family for being prime examples of successfully doing their own thing—and doing it with style, humor, optimism, and intelligent planning.

PREFACE

I know a secret, and over the years have shared it with countless engineers, directors, managers, teachers, programmers, civil service employees, high school graduates, clerks, presidents, and people from all walks of life.

The secret involves a better way to find a better job. The friends and business associates who successfully utilized this approach found their lives, ambitions, job satisfaction, and incomes changed dramatically for the better.

In terms of their career skills they all had something to offer, but didn't know how to market it. This led to a terrible waste of their talent in general, and a frustrated career and life in particular. Until they tried the secret. In every case they have thanked me and immediately asked, "Why don't you write a book so more people can have their lives made more worthwhile?"

I finally took the hint!

So, relax and get comfortable: here comes an exciting learning experience. You are going to learn something about:

Who you are
Where you want to go

What the best strategies are for finding a new position
When to use the best specific tactics or techniques
How to market yourself—with a plan, hard-working and effective materials, job targets, plus interviewing and negotiating strategies.

In job hunting there is a job to do and learn, not a crisis that has no end. Don't give in to panic, despair, frustration, anger, or depression. Be prepared to have these normal feelings, just don't give in to them.

Note: through all of this, there may be a few places where "he" or other male references are used. If so, it's just for the sake of saving some time and ink, and should be interpreted as "he *or* she." All of these job-finding techniques have been successfully used by both men and women for many years.

A final word of advice: do not jump into the job market before you are ready. You have to pay some dues first. You don't want to spoil your chances with any prime contacts or leads before you learn how to handle yourself with cunning wit, style, flair, intelligence, and consummate skill. So read on!

BURTON E. LIPMAN

East Brunswick, N.J.
March 1983

HOW TO USE THIS BOOK

For the overly impatient, who insist on jumping before they are ready, there is a resume and letter-writing crash course in Chapters 10 through 13. You probably won't get the job that way, but it will help you produce much better written materials.

The preferred approach is to read through the entire book to understand the step-by-step development of the Program; then go back and put the individual job-search strategies into effect.

CONTENTS

O N E

INTRODUCTION TO JOB HUNTING

S tart from reality and strength: you are entitled to be optimistic, because somewhere out there is the right job for you. You are entitled to self-confidence, because there is no one else in the world with your particular assortment of abilities. You deserve to have self-esteem, since no one is perfect and you are as worthy or as entitled to live and grow on this planet as anyone else.

You do have many strong points, be it your education, experience, job know-how, business intuition, intelligence, honesty, or your ability to analyze, sell, scheme, or write. Successful people come in all types and sizes. So, it's just fine if you are a pessimist or an optimist, shy or outgoing, entrepreneureal or bureaucratic, instinctive or slow to analyze, male or female, brown-noser or fearless leader, young or old, thinker or doer, detail-oriented or big-picture thinker, stubborn or flexible, daydreamer or a hard-nosed business person.

There is room for everyone out there, because the endless variety of jobs, companies, departments, and bosses ensures that everyone and anyone can ultimately find a suitable job.

The above optimism is the first "reality" you should know, accept, and believe. Next is the need to translate this belief into self-confidence. That can yield a positive attitude towards your search program; an attitude of winning that literally becomes a self-fulfilling prophecy.

Even if you were just fired, or are stuck in a dead-end job, accept this stage of your career as just that: a temporary period of learning, growing, exploring, and opportunity-seeking. This is a rare opportunity indeed, an *ideal* time to take stock of yourself and your goals, where you have been and where you would like to go.

The next reality is: you won't find that right job by next Tuesday. Job hunting is not an overnight process. To do it right requires learning about yourself, the job market, how to plan a campaign, preparing and testing your tools and skills, and mounting an effective, targeted campaign.

3

Most of your competitors in this race for the perfect job will be less skilled, less prepared, and less effective than you. They may be better executives or managers or scientists, but *you* will have a tested, right-for-you marketing campaign that shifts the odds radically in your favor. But there is still plenty of competition that is answering every ad you are answering—so it usually takes practice and a number of tries before the odds can begin paying off in your favor.

Basic Job-Finding Rules

No matter what your profession or experience level, these four rules are essential to job finding success.

The First Rule: Timing—It's Never Too Early to Start

The best time to look for a new job is when you don't need one.

1. You then have available, valuable *time;*
2. You are gainfully employed, with no threat of unemployment;
3. With sufficient time to think about your career objectives;
4. To adequately plan your strategies and prepare the necessary tools (letters, resumes);
5. To strengthen your base of operations: to build the type of background and *exposure* that will make offers come to you;
6. To reflect on and correct those personal *behavior* characteristics that have gotten you into trouble in the past;
7. To figure out how you can stay tuned-in to the *political* wars, and end up on the winning side the next time there's a political power struggle;

8. To figure out how to be considered *essential* the next time there is a *cutback;*
9. To plan how you can stay on your *boss's "team"*; and
10. To learn how to better lead and develop your own staff.

The Second Rule: Play Hard-to-Get

This is a derivative of the first rule: Act as if time is on your side. Thus, always play hard-to-get. Act independent and self-confident, in good, subdued taste, of course. It's tough to pull this off successfully when you are out of a job, or are so discontented that you can't help racing after every new job opening at full speed. But begging for a job, or appearing to, just doesn't work. That's why you should try to start your search before you desperately need a job. You can relax, be confident, and play hard-to-get in a natural way.

Playing hard-to-get sends out another signal that basically you are happy and adjusted (but always interested in a new challenge). After all, no company wants a malcontent, a cast-off, or a misfit. That's why no company is particularly attracted to you if you are out of work; you'll seem to be too much of a risk somehow, even if the reason for unemployment is not your fault.

Certainly no headhunter will want to recommend you to his clients if you appear too eager or will go with "anybody." Recruiters play a selling game all their own; that's their business: "We can get that perfect fit for you, Mr. Corporate Client, that one best candidate you could never reach, who is currently doing a productive job and who normally wouldn't think of leaving." The Recruiter's implied promise is "We won't send you one of the thousands of job-seekers now pounding the sidewalk and deluging you with resumes. We'll get you the very best, with great secrecy, no matter where they are, and even if they are not looking." It's mostly a sales pitch, of course, since almost everyone looks around in the job market during their career.

Nevertheless, you must show the recruiters that you are attuned and sensitive enough to respect the headhunting image they are trying to project for themselves and the candidates they offer. Thus, the approach to them should be somewhat hard-to-get: "I'm productively employed now, but I might be willing to listen to any challenging opportunities that could help in furthering my long-term goals." Play it cool. If they want you, they won't be turned off by this response. It should actually whet their interest in you!

The Third Rule: Don't Blow All Your Best Chances on Day One

If you haven't redrafted your resume at least three times, you're not really trying. Nothing ever goes perfectly, particularly the first few times. That's why plays have rehearsals and out-of-town openings: to try out.

Moral: don't waste a prime target with a half-baked resume on the first day. Wait until you get your act together before playing the Palace.

The Fourth Rule: Be a Known Quantity!

Read the next chapter and see why this is positively the most important rule of all!

T W O
THE SECRET
OF SUCCESS

You are probably scheming, worrying, or otherwise thinking about the job during 80% of your waking hours. With your emotional investment this high, the misfortune of being slotted in the wrong job, department, or company—or working for the wrong boss—can ruin your entire working life. You don't have to be a victim of such a fate. You don't have to settle for a career and a life that is not a true match for your personal goals and capabilities. Thus, don't swap the testing of your mettle for "security"; life is too short to "waste" any of your time.

Moral one
You deserve—and can find—challenge and fulfillment!

Life Is a Game . . .

Over the years I have known a broad cross section of professionals throughout the personnel field. They are mostly bright and very astute observers (albeit not participants), of the bathos, pathos, high-tragedy and the low-comedy-filled game called "How to get ahead in business." I share their innermost reactions to this game: a five- to ten-percent mix of cynicism, with the overwhelming balance composed of laughter, a sense of humor, and a fascination with the career game's endless variations of human ambition, best-laid plans, the fickle finger of fate, pratfalls, and all of the self-defeating kindergarten games that pass for office politics and other get-ahead strategies.

Moral two
Life is a game. So, too, is your career—play it as a free spirit. Your sense of humor must have as its principle "don't take your job, or yourself, too seriously." You can play the game (of life or career) most successfully if you relax and play the game with humor and optimism.

The "Getting Ahead" Game

Over the course of many years, I have heard hundreds of career stories about how people get jobs, why people get fired, and what experienced headhunters and other personnel people would do if they needed a job.

The stories are as varied as the people they involve. Some are as fateful as a Greek tragedy, and in other cases as hilarious as your favorite comedian's monologue, and yet they all contain an underlying set of principles that apply equally to Ph.Ds, high-school dropouts, Yale graduates, teachers, clerks, and corporate presidents.

1. Most people find and get their jobs through pull, connections, or knowing someone.
2. Most people want to leave—or actually lose—their jobs because of "no-fault" personality conflicts with a boss.
3. The best way to get a new job is to become thought of as a Known Quantity, even if it's only on a very remote and tenuous "pull" basis.

The Big Secret

In my conversations with personnel experts I always asked: "If *you* were suddenly forced to find another job, what would you do first?" The invariable answer is "Open my desk's center drawer and grab my stack of business cards that I've collected from everyone I know. Next, I'd pick out a few companies that I'd really like to work for. The rest is simple; I'd call around until I got someone who could get me a lead inside one of my target companies. If that's pull or 'knowing someone,' who cares—because it works!"

"Ha," you say, "none of this is fair, equitable, or just!" You, gentle reader, are quite correct, but unrealistic, too! Read on:

1. Having connections or "pull" *is* discriminatory and un-democratic. But it's also a universal and historical fact of life, and probably always will be.

2. Being fired doesn't seem very fair, particularly if it's due to a no-fault, everyday personality conflict. But if you are (a) unhappy with your present job, or (b) about to be fired, it's neither a great tragedy nor a sin. Life is too short to endure constant grief, so go gladly forth and aggressively seek your fortune. Don't do it every six months, though; that's a problem, too!

It may not be "right" if you get a job merely because you are a known quantity, perhaps only a "friend of a friend of a friend," but it happens every day. And that is an immutable fact of life.

Moral three

If you want to survive, no matter what fate has handed you, you must actively fight back. That means become a Known Quantity!

This book is unconventional. So far, you are soberly sitting there and wondering:

1. "Is that all the author has for me? It's no big deal or big secret."

2. "If I had any pull, I wouldn't know how to use it."

3. "I don't even believe in using pull."

4. "This book's approach is facile and superficial: it is to-tally unlike the conventional wisdom found in those job-finding books that all the experts write and all the job-seekers read."

In regard to observations 1 and 2: The principles are simple but you do need to learn how to develop pull. As for point 3:

This book will attempt to convince you to believe in the pragmatic power of pull, and show you how to use it in finding a new job, no matter what your current circumstances may be.

As for point 4: this book *is* contrary to conventional wisdom. The usual approach to career counselors, outplacement specialists, and the typical books on the subject consists of:

How to write a good resume and cover letter

How to mail these out in a broadcast campaign to recruiters and companies, and

How to conduct yourself in an interview.

The conventional result is: Every known headhunter in the land receives hundreds of unsolicited resumes in the mail every working day from strangers he has never heard of. Every large company likewise receives a continuous flood of resumes from unknowns each day. Every attractive ad is answered by hundreds of job seekers, using strikingly similar cover letters and smartly printed resumes.

This is the Mail-a-Million approach: it is the conventional and well-trod path that almost everyone automatically adopts when they decide to seek a new position. And yet, it is *not* an approach that is responsive to the hirer's anxious world of "I don't really know you . . . Who *are* you?" These scatter-gun mailing campaigns result in every candidate being in the same boat: they all become faceless unknowns with no one standing out in the crowd.

The next question we must now answer is, if the conventional approach is so overworked and misses the real-world needs of the hirer, why is it so widely practiced, preached, and written about?

I can't fully explain this phenomenon. It's undoubtedly a combination of inertia, the unimaginative following of everyone else, a misguided belief that quantity can overcome the law of averages in finding a job, and the over-eager efforts of some experts to give all of you inexperienced, shy, and scared job seekers an easy and nonthreatening way to approach the job market. With all your contacts done by mail, it does spare you the personal terror and psychological trauma of being rejected on a face-to-face basis.

The Best Way

If you were a boss trying to make a hiring decision, you would likely select a candidate that you have confidence in: someone who has been vouched for personally by someone whose judgment you know.

This book can teach you how to become that vouched-for leading candidate, no matter how small you think your circle of influential friends may be. We also cover the basics: Setting your career goals, writing effective resumes and letters, how to use a mail campaign to sharpen and test your approach, and how to interview and negotiate your starting salary.

You deserve a shot at challenge and success—and this book can show you how to achieve it.

How to Do It

The first step in your job search project is to understand and prepare for what's ahead. Career advancement is a big job, requiring a plan of action, testing of the plan, the setting of objectives and a lot of serious preparation time.

Don't think there exists a secret key to success or a magic short cut to this important task. In fact, there is no one best way; timing, good luck, being in the right place, and knowing someone all play a major part. But proper planning and preparation will shift the odds in your favor. As in all major undertakings, we must plan the work—and work the plan. Anything else is trusting to dumb luck.

What we will do first in this book is to get you in touch with reality: the job market, your real goals, and the pitfalls that you must be aware of (and that, once you know what they are, you can avoid).

Then, we will help you design a plan that gives you the best shot at the job you seek, whether you are a first timer, have already tried and failed in the job market, are suddenly unemployed, or want to look around on a confidential basis.

Next, we cover the overall strategy for your jobfinding campaign, and tell you what to do first, which items are for rehearsing or "testing" purposes, and which tactics are most likely to help you succeed.

After reading the tactics section, those readers with a resume and a stack of postage stamps already in hand may feel the urge to mail out those 200 or 2,000 letters and resumes tomorrow. Resist the temptation—read the whole book first.

Finally, we cover the upbeat portions of your campaign: how to negotiate your new salary, and the elements of true job security.

Before we start, let's cover one important item right here: taxes.

Tax Tip

The expense involved in finding a new job may be deductible on your personal income tax. This includes printing, mailing, and telephone costs, and travel involved in finding a new position. The regulations do change, so check the latest set of IRS and state tax rules. Let Uncle Sam help you in your job search! Just make sure you keep detailed expense records.

T H R E E

WHO ARE YOU?

Y ou are now going to determine your strengths and interests, to build your self awareness of your individual skills. When you get done, you hopefully won't categorize yourself any longer as "just an accountant" or grandly give your major interest as, "I like working with people."

First Step: Major Accomplishments

List at least 25 of your accomplishments during your total career. Nearly everyone has accomplished more than he or she realizes. Before you bang out that resume, use these steps to reevaluate your own accomplishments—you'll be surprised at just how good you are.

1. Start with the earliest ones, no matter how small. Do not neglect the obvious (for example getting toilet devices to conserve water, or clipping *Wall Street Journal* articles applying to your business and tacking them up at work or giving them to the boss, etc.).
2. Tell what you did and what it saved or improved.
3. Start each accomplishment with an action word: reduced/achieved/created/sold/implemented are all good, grabbing sentence starters.

Write them out—right now—with dollar-savings or other specifics.

Examples:

Saved $300,000 in direct labor costs by installing new standards.
Increased employee productivity by 25% through improved scheduling.
Reduced inventory by $250,000 through new control system.

Organized sales force training, resulting in 30% less turnover and 40% increased sales.

Negotiated two labor agreements with no work stoppages.

Reduced accounts receivable by 60% within 12 months.

Upgraded old-fashioned product line; reversed falling sales and profits.

Formulated new order-processing procedures, reduced fulfillment cycle by 28%.

Developed a new laboratory organization: eliminated $150,-000 of duplication.

Identified new product markets for division, which resulted in line expansion, and diversification into related equipment.

Improved unfavorable variance from 40% to less than 5% within one year.

Prepared promotional flyers for 80 different products.

Created . . . cost controls . . . that saved . . .

Introduced . . . into a new market . . .

Promoted/cut/installed/designed . . .

Second Step: Priorities

1. Put priority numbers in the margin of your own list of accomplishments, based on how proud you are and/or how much you enjoyed working on each. Your proudest and most satisfying entry will be number one, for example.

2. Based on your top-priority items, make a preliminary list of the types of work you like to do that reflect the projects and accomplishments that are at or near the top of your priority list.

3. *Preference List*   Put the priority list aside for now, and dream up answers, in writing, to the following questions:

Do I want to remain in my field?

Am I qualified to do other jobs?

Do I want to become qualified to do other jobs? Should I start to plan or train now?

What are my short-term and long-term career goals?

If I have a choice, do I want to stay with my current employer?

Do I prefer a large or small organization?

Do I enjoy my current job?

Did I enjoy my last job? prior jobs?

Which job(s) did I enjoy the most? the least?

Do I want more security and less pressure?

How important is salary? title?

What does my family want?

What are my performance (and personality) assets and liabilities?

What type of company do I prefer: Profit or non-profit; manufacturing or service; retail or distribution; international or domestic; headquarters or divisional staff; centralized or decentralized? What basic industry: insurance or fast food; steel or chemicals; banking or my own business?

What geographic location preferences do I have? What would it take to lure me to a new location?

4. Stop reading right now if you have not yet sat down, picked up a pencil or pen, found some paper, and done your homework. I can't fill out your First Step accomplishment list, your Next Step principles, or your answers to the list of 15 preference questions. If you want to pay a counselor a large fee to read these types of questions off to you, go ahead and spend your money. Otherwise, get to work right now.

5. The prioritized accomplishment list and your preference
    list answers should form a rough pattern of who you are,
    what you like, and where you want to go. Study them
    and find that pattern of career satisfaction. You should
    be able to learn about your management style, and,
    most importantly, become aware of what you can do
    that you should be proud of. This exercise is bound to
    improve your self-esteem and confidence.

This is your golden opportunity, a watershed period, a
chance to pick the right fork in the road: it's all these good
things, so *do* it. Here's your chance to restore satisfaction in
your work! Now write down your first, second, and third
choices of company/title/location.

Be Happy in Your Work

You probably ended up in your present industry or field of en-
deavor by accident. Perhaps you'll be happier doing something
else, a new career in a different industry. Maybe the political
climate of most companies is not to your liking; you find it
hard to cope with authority, or you can't stand corporate
bureaucracies.

If this is so, you will not find permanent happiness if you
merely get that next raise, or that next promotion, or that new
job with your company's competitor.

Examine your working career: where and when were you
most happy, challenged, and satisfied? Would you be happier
in business for yourself? large or small company? line or staff?
sales or accounting? The list goes on and on.

If you are convinced that you are merely a temporarily mis-
placed person, career-wise, you can skip the rest of this section.
But, if a career-switch seems appealing, start now to investi-
gate. Sure, there may be some short-term reasons for not
changing right now, perhaps heavy family or financial obliga-

tions. In the meantime, you may have to settle for a move within your current career.

However, no matter what circumstances you're experiencing, you can start planning and preparing now. Take a course that could further your job interests, join a club or association, start a hobby that has business-development possibilities, or relocate geographically if that is part of your ultimate plan.

You say you haven't the time to do any of these things, or the money, either? That's no excuse. Head over to your local library and read up on your new career, correspond with others in your newly chosen field, or start saving money to get yourself financially prepared for the change.

Go for the Good Jobs

Some managers make a career out of helping the financial "turnaround" of troubled companies. The excitement and challenge is personally appealing to these managers. But, such companies are not normally in a staff-expansion frame of mind, so statistically you may be better off looking for a position or choosing a career in a growth area or industry. (Of course, if everyone does that, it makes it easier for you to get one of the few turnaround jobs in depressed industries, if that is what appeals to you.)

As a general rule, however, read the *Wall Street Journal,* government reports, trade and general business magazines: you might as well go where the good jobs are geographically, industry and company-wise, and career-wise. Certain jobs and industries are in decline; others are in a long-term growth phase such as the service fields, communications, computer-related fields, food-related fields, sales, and health care.

Also look for the leaders in each field, particularly in the early phases of your career. Such companies will give you first-rate experience, and they normally promote from within.

Thus, avoid companies that are in a rut, whose sales or market share is slipping, where five years of experience could turn out to be "one year's experience repeated five times." Long tenure with poorly run companies also does not add much to your luster or professionalism when listed on your resume.

The choice is clearly yours: be happy in your career, wherever that may lead you. But, as the saying goes, it's often just as easy to love a rich person as a poor one.

You are in charge of yourself! You can do almost anything you set your heart on. Don't just sit there, take yourself where you really want to go. You deserve happiness, and you'll do better all around if you enjoy what you are doing. Life is too short not to be happy in your work.

F O U R

THE JOB MARKET

The managerial job market is unorganized, chaotic, and dreadfully inefficient. On the one side are thousands of companies looking for the most suitable candidates, and on the other are thousands of anxious candidates seeking a suitable position. There is no common meeting ground, no central clearing house, no unified referral system, no impartial national service. With no method to all this randomness, many techniques are used to bring the parties together, most of them ad hoc, local, parochial, or worse. Here are the leading tactics used by companies to find you, their ideal candidate.

Tactics Used by Companies to Fill Openings

1. Promote an underling from within: a known quantity.
2. Transfer and promote from within: transfer in a somewhat known quantity from a different department.
3. Pursue leads by personal contact, referrals, or by approaching a known candidate in another company. Each of these candidates is thus a known quantity, at least by referral.
4. Run a positions available ad.
5. Spread the word: Make the opening known to industry-association leaders, bankers, suppliers who call on the industry, fellow executives in their own or other companies, and other business associates.
6. List the job with one or more employment agencies.
7. Hire an executive recruiter to search out the ideal candidate.
8. Start reading the flood of unsolicited resumes that are received daily by the company.
9. Maybe, just maybe, dig into the files of past unsolicited resumes that someone in Personnel had been keeping "just in case."

Depending on the company, and the circumstances, the employer's choice of tactics will vary widely. However, in general, companies often adhere to the percentages of this example:

		Usual Percent Ranges	
		Middle Level	Top Level Job
1.	Promote underling	50–90%	60–90%
2.	Promotion from other department	13–40	15–40
3.	Personal contact, referral or approach known outside candidate	12–30	10–30
4.	Run company's ad	10–30	5–20
5.	Spread word	0–5	5–20
6.	Use agency	10–30	0–5
7.	Hire recruiter	5–20	5–30
8.	Read incoming resumes	0–25	0–25
9.	Read old resume file	0–3	0–2
10.	Answer "Position Wanted" ad	—	—

Reading the Odds

That's a great little table, if it is to be believed. It tells you almost all you have to know about which tactics you should use, in order to become their suitable candidate. For example, for most jobs, this particular table says that you should concentrate on:

Inside promotion (be a Known Quantity!)
Personal contacts (be a Known Quantity!)

Answering ads
Employment agencies (perhaps)
Executive recruiters
Write to companies directly (maybe)

In other words, don't rely solely on the usual or easy way of mail-a-million resumes to ads, agencies, or recruiters. Also, forget the other techniques that don't usually work: writing thousands of impersonal Dear Sir letters to companies, or running your own job-wanted ad.

You need personal and business contacts, and a well-thought-out plan to develop and use them. Look for where the jobs are, have a plan, and go after them.

Selecting Your Strategies

The specific strategies you should use in your job search depend on who you are and where you want to go. There is a whole range of options open to you, a supermarket full of different strategies for you to pick and choose. This section will provide specific guidance on how to sort them out.

Job-Hunting Strategies

1. Search inside your present company.
2. Ask your firm for outplacement assistance, if you are asked to leave.
3. Write broadcast letters to many companies and head-hunters.
4. Answer ads in papers and industry magazines.
5. Write or call professional associations: your college placement office, professional societies, and so on.

6.   Write to companies known to be in trouble, and to executives who have been hired recently; offer to join their (new) team.

7.   Narrow down step 3: Write only to companies in your choice of industry, geographic area, companies of a certain size, and so on.

8.   Register with some employment agencies.

9.   Ask your friends for job leads.

10.   Ask your business acquaintances for leads.

11.   Select target companies or headhunters. Attempt to get a personal or business contact reference inside the company. Call or write to the contact.

12.   Visit state employment agency.

13.   Run your own "position wanted" ad.

14.   Visit company plant or headquarters, fill out applications.

15.   Spend some significant up-front money to hire an executive placement, counseling, or resume-writing firm to write your resume and perhaps give you interview tips and a mailing list.

Plan Your Priorities

For any job seeker, from beginner to top level, I strongly suggest you follow the above 15 strategies in the same order as they are presented, with the following provisos and explanations.

1.   *Search inside.*   No explanation necessary. Always look inside first.

2.   *Outplacement.*   If you are confident in your job search abilities, you may not want to press too hard for an outplacement service; ask instead for severance pay or staying on the payroll "in lieu. . . ."

3. *Big mailings.* Don't go overboard on large-scale mailings; consider them as a test or an exercise to see how well your letters and resumes are working. Also, don't count too heavily on this approach; that is, don't spend all your capital (money *or* morale) on these tests. Think in terms of 50 or 100, not 500 or 1,000.

   If you hit the jackpot and get a job, fine. If not, there are many other strategies you can try—this is a test, after all.

4. *Answering ads.* This is one way to practice your writing skills. But don't build up your hopes too high—this is normally a long shot.

5 & 6. *Professional associations/companies in trouble/newly hired executives.* This is a good exercise, but not guaranteed to work. (They have *all* worked for me, so don't go strictly by the overall odds.)

7. *Narrow down your mailing list.* You have tested your materials and are now ready to tackle more serious possibilities. But don't poison your most desirable targets yet with halfbaked resumes and no personal pull. Save those most promising, hard to get, but delicious possibilities for Step 11—your targeted strategy for success!

Warning: Don't be afraid if you do happen to get a decent job offer during steps 1 to 10. Before accepting, run a crash campaign against your favorite targets, and see if you can't duplicate your success. If there is time, try the Step 11 "known quantity" approach—you have one good offer, now try for a better one.

8. *Employment agencies.* At lower levels, try some agencies.

9 & 10. *Ask for leads.* Get all the leads you can, but read this entire book before you misuse or abuse them. You

should do these steps *only* to prepare for strategy 11: it's your best shot.

11. *Become a known quantity inside your target companies.* This is the strategy that gets the most jobs outside your present company. It is covered in depth in this book.

12. *State employment agencies.* These are useful primarily for unskilled jobs.

13. *Position-wanted ads.* These don't work as a very general but well-proven rule.

14. *Visiting companies to fill out applications.* This is normally a waste of time, except for unskilled jobs.

15. *Get professional aid.* Unless you have lots of disposable money and are in dire need of psychological hand-holding and expensive resume-writing aid, try reading this book first.

Company Hiring Strategies vs. Your Job-Hunting Strategies

Elsewhere we spelled out how you can compute the odds, based on the hiring strategies that a company may use. This approach is strictly a guess and, further, there are exceptions to everything. After all, some people are offered the job only because they are six feet tall, or have red hair, or have a father on the board of directors. That's why you can take such suggestions with a grain of salt, unless you have some hard information that makes you an informed guesser.

To help sort this all out, I strongly recommend that you take the previous 15 strategies (and their provisos) in the exact order I have listed them. They are amplified upon in the following chapters, so don't stop reading yet. Some individual-circumstance variations may be called for; two are outlined here.

Strategy Variation 1: Recent High School Graduate

Move up employment agencies (8) to position 3.
Move up friend's job leads (9) to position 4.

Strategy Variation 2: Women Newly Reentering the Work Force

Move up college placement and societies (5) to position 1.
Move up employment agencies (8) to position 2 (primarily to get an updated feel for the market).

Otherwise, you should follow these 15 strategies in the order given. Strategy 1 must always be tried first. Strategy 11 is the best for outside jobs, but strategies 3, 4, 5, 6, 7, 8, 9 and 10 are all useful, all potentially successful, and are all necessary steps to prepare you for strategy 11. They are the testing, learning, and skill-building steps to your successful job search!

One last point: we won't overlook any opportunity in this book, including the conventional approaches. (After all, steps numbered 3, 4, 7 and 8 are the conventional steps.) But we use them for two purposes:

1. To help find a job, perhaps early in your search.
2. To *also* use as necessary learning steps to build a solid and successful search program.

Keeping Your Search Confidential

If you are currently employed and don't want your employer to learn of your job search activities, some discretion is called for:

1. Be careful whom you contact or take into your confidence.

2. Be extra wary if you see an attractive blind ad with only a box number and no clues as to which company it might be.

3. Be careful in contacting employment agencies: some of them may be working closely with your present company and your name might somehow get back to your boss.

This still leaves many other search options open to you, although none of them are guaranteed to be 100% safe. Writing directly to other companies seems safe enough, but there is always that rare chance that the recipient is a personal friend of someone in your company.

Since there is always some risk, just try to minimize it. For example, when contacting executive recruiters, try to use those who are members of the Association of Executive Recruiting Consultants (AERC), or who subscribe to their code of professional ethics.

On your resume, you may want to disguise the identity of your current company, such as: "A Fortune 500 consumer goods company."

Maintain the Appearance of Being Employed

If you have recently left a company, and want to keep the appearance of being currently employed you should continue to use the disguised company identity on your resume, as described in the previous paragraph, unless the company's name and reputation would be a real plus to your resume's selling impact.

As a general rule, unless you are fresh out of school, you should always try to keep up the appearance of still being employed as far as your letters and resumes are concerned. Potential hirers who will scan your resume don't like people who are out of work. Thus, the discreet, continued use of your resume that specifically indicates your last job has been worked from the starting date up to "the present" is the usual practice for not turning off a prospective hirer. You can (and should) always explain your most current status during the interview. But first things first—you need to get that interview.

If you have been unemployed for a relatively long period of time, consider doing some freelance or part-time business consulting, and listing that as your current position. Any time gaps in your resume will be disturbing to a prospective hirer. This is doubly true when the time gap is for the current period!

PITFALLS
TO AVOID

W e will now point out the pitfalls to avoid along the pathway to finding a new job. Everyone who has ever tested the job market has fallen into these hidden traps, diversions, and obstacles. So be warned in advance! (If any of this already has happened to you, read it twice.)

1. "I tried to do it on a part-time or once-over-lightly basis."

   Answer: Job hunting requires commitment and the solid investment of your time. In fact, it could be one of the most important jobs of your working career.

2. "I got discouraged—I looked for a month without results."

   Answer: A well-executed plan takes time to draw up, test until it's right, and execute properly.

3. "I read a book, wrote a resume and cover letter as suggested, and mailed out 500 of them. Got no positive responses."

   Answer: Perhaps you read a just-copy-me resume-writing book. Or worse, maybe you skipped some of the hard parts in one of the better books, like the self-analysis, the telephone scripts, or the research on target companies. If so, don't skip the tough parts of this book: no author can do it all for you! If you do it all, and study it all, then you can do some informed testing; it may be just a correctable flaw in your resume that's the current problem.

4. "I got discouraged—I had a really good resume and answered 20 ads and wrote to 50 companies and 30 headhunters, and got no results."

   Answer: Here's another reality, mentioned briefly in an earlier chapter: the same day your resume arrived, so did 200 others! The law of averages is against you on each try. The best answers are: have outstanding materials (letter, resume, etc.) and have a defined plan that is targeted specifically toward companies and recruiters who might need your particular assets today. So, recognize the longshot odds you face on each try, and keep trying with your best shot.

5.   "I'm getting some offers, but they are from companies that are too small or too large/are in the wrong industry/are for jobs that are not in my field/or are for jobs that are too low-paying."

Answer: Are you following a plan that is aimed directly at the right-sized companies in the right industries for a job at the right level in the right field? Make sure your written materials reflect the job you really want. If you did a haphazard job on your self-evaluation, chances are good that your stated personal objective is not specific. You could then be ignored easily, or offered the wrong type of job. This is wasteful and expensive.

Keep your spirits up: the fact that you are getting some answers is a good reflection on the overall quality of your approach.

6.   "I sent out 200 letters to leading companies and then another 500, but I really am only interested in about six of them. I'm not having too much success—nothing of real interest . . ."

Answer: This is another extremely commonplace pitfall, and it has two answers:

> You are still using the "mass-mailing" mind-set of job hunting strategy that so many others try without success.

> You should be researching/targeting/pursuing your six favorites!

7.   "I just got fired, and I don't know what to do."

Answer: This is such a common situation today that it is nothing to be ashamed of. The problems of relocating are more difficult if unemployed, but there is more time available to overcome them.

The next chapter is devoted entirely to the subject of unemployment—don't despair.

8. "In my last interview, my smoking (or loud tie/beard/excuse for being late/excuse for leaving my last company/sloppy application form/unawareness of the products or sales dollars of the company) seemed to bother the person who interviewed me. Too bad! I have a lot on my mind, many things to do, and I'm not changing myself just to give in to them."

Answer: It's not a question of giving in—interviewing is a long-standing formalized ritual that gives a quick snapshot of who you are. Smoking or otherwise distracting the proceedings, or being unprepared, can only poison the atmosphere. Be realistic! Don't constantly repeat your foibles—purposefully discard them, for the first interview at least. This doesn't mean you have to sacrifice your personality, or put on an interview mask—pretending to be someone you're not only hurts. What this does mean is that you have to market yourself and make yourself an attractive candidate.

9. "I'm too shy to use my friends or business pals as contacts. I don't want them to know I'm unhappy (or fired). And even if they give me someone's name, I wouldn't know what to do with it."

Answer: Just remember the odds you are up against as an unknown:

The majority of higher-level jobs are filled by people who are already personally known or referred to the employer's decision-makers.

The decision-maker may even *make* a job for a "known quantity."

To get the odds to work more in your favor, you must face the fact that sending out 1,000 or even 2,000 resumes is comparatively ineffective, time-wasting, and expensive, even if it helps you save face with your friends, or spares you the imagined trauma of face-to-face pleading, arm-twisting, personal selling, or cold-calling.

There is a way to get the odds working in your favor. It's outlined in this book. Your self-analysis will help build your self-confidence, and these two ingredients will enable you to write a good resume, which again will build your self-image. You can then test your resume, brush up on interviewing, and be ready, willing, and able to tap your primary resources: business and personal contacts. In the meantime, your preliminary resume mailings may also get you some interviews, leads, or offers.

In other words, you can have the best of both worlds!

You Can Beat the Odds

Theorems.
1. More is not always better than less.
2. Quantity doesn't always overcome lack of quality.
3. If you want to beat the averages, don't bet on a horse— own the paramutual machine.

Comments.   Mailing 100 resumes won't get you 100 job offers. Your only returns may be from the post office: "unable to deliver." This costs much more than mailing 1 or 10, and the results of 100 may still be zero. In addition, this has now become a gamble where the law of averages doesn't help you much, because *everyone* is now mailing out hundreds! However, quality does count. So we will cover the art of presenting yourself properly using resumes and letters.

Now comes the best part: beating the law of averages. Up to 90% of the good job openings never are published. They go instead to people who have an inside track; they have an entree, an advantage, they are known quantities. Let the rest of the world fight over the 10% that ends up with agencies, headhunters, or in ads. You will reach for the biggest and best jobs where, paradoxically, the competition is the least.

A List of Don'ts

1. Don't think you can get a job without connections. Sure, it's possible, but at higher levels it's a long shot. Consider how many hundreds of people will be answering that same ad for a job, or writing "Dear Sir" letters.

2. Don't think you can get a job if you merely "mail a million" resumes. It's another long shot. If you are a known quantity, he already knows who you are and what you can and cannot do.

3. Don't think you have nothing to lose by answering dozens of ads or by making gigantic mailings. You *can* lose:

    valuable time;

    valuable effort;

    valuable momentum and morale if you are counting too heavily on these overworked vehicles; and

    a lot of money as well, just on printing and postage costs. Being a known quantity might only cost you a single phone call!

The Moral Issue.   There is nothing sinister, immoral, or illegal about all this if you understand the game and its rules.

Most people are *fired* because of personality clashes rather than lack of expertise, and

It's also true that bosses prefer to deal with a known quantity when *filling* a position. A candidate's personality quotient is the dimension that bosses are the most uneasy dealing with. It's the dimension that a half-hour, or even a three-hour interview cannot be relied upon to measure, unravel, or judge with any degree of accuracy. That's a very understandable and natural reaction. Thus, there's nothing wrong with playing the game. Just become a known quantity, and win!

Avoidance of Rejection

Be warned: it's too easy to do what every other job seeker does:

1. Dash off a resume and a universal cover letter, and then:
2. Answer newspaper ads.
3. Write to 300 headhunters (executive recruiters).
4. Write to 200 companies.
5. Perhaps register with one or more employment agencies.
6. Maybe consider running a job-wanted ad.

This features no self-evaluation, no company targeting, no time-consuming research into the companies, no targeting of tactics, and usually, no offers, either. Its attraction is not just laziness: it's a non-threatening way of avoiding face-to-face *rejection!*

Often, all you get is silence, no answers, or a stack of form letters that politely say "nothing is available now, but your background looks interesting and your materials will be kept on file in case something ever does open up." All very civilized, sanitized, computerized, but not very helpful. Thus, the real problems of the so-called easy way are that even though it avoids some face-to-face embarrassment, it is an ineffective tactic. There must be a personalized, targeted plan, not just thousands of letters. That only makes the post office rich, not you.

SIX

IN CASE
OF FIRE

D on't quit if you can possibly avoid it. Try to hang in there even if your boss is a sadist, your desk was just moved into the stairwell, your salary was cut, the secretaries stare at you, or your job "is to be eliminated." Unless there is a life-threatening or health-threatening reason, do not quit.

The reason is simple: it is always easier to find another job, inside or outside the company, if you are still employed. Prospective employers always figure that if you are currently employed, someone thinks you can do a job and are worth a salary. It's the first, if not the primary reference they rely upon.

But if you are fired or asked to resign, be prepared to act fast. Once you are out the door, you can't ask for anything except a reference. If you are still on the premises, you have some cards to play. There is usually some flexibility involved, so you must have a ready list of requests. Here is your ready-made checklist.

1. Instead of "severance today and leave," ask to stay on the payroll for at least the period covered by any severance pay. This way, you can safely tell prospective employers that you are currently employed. This also will continue your insurance and other benefits for a while.

2. In any case, ask that your benefits be continued for three to six months "until you relocate."

3. Whether or not officially on the payroll, ask if you can have the use of an office, secretary, and/or telephone to "help you ease the relocation."

4. Ask for someone to take messages and mail for you, while you are "out of the office."

5. Get agreement on a suitable public reason or announcement for the "resignation."

6. Request a job interview with a department head in a different sector of the company.

7. Request a company-paid "outplacement program" given by the personnel department, or preferably by a leading consulting company in the field. If you feel confident that you really don't need this, ask for it less strongly, and if there is any guilt on the company's part (there usually is), immediately ask for three month's additional severance in lieu of the cost of such a program.

8. Ask if you can continue to be active in any company-sponsored industry associations, to keep up your contacts, and your image.

9. Request a full explanation of the status of all fringes: various insurance coverages, any vesting rights or cash values or conversion privileges. Ask for official conversion forms, and written copies of your retirement or other benefits.

10. Make a list of the personal items in your office, and make arrangements to take them home or to have them be sent to your home.

11. If there are any reasons for special pay or other considerations, bring them up quickly:

    (a) Were you moved to a geographic area far from your home base?

    (b) Were you promised a bonus or other consideration?

    (c) Can you continue to use your company car until you "get settled?"

    (d) Are you in such a specialized industry or job function that it will take you six months longer than normal to find another position?

    (e) If you originally came in as part of a high-risk turnaround situation, stress the fact that you had assumed all along that they would help protect you if it didn't work out.

(f) If you are a long-term employee, or have per-
sonal/family problems, ask for consideration on
that basis. If long-term, ask for at *least* one week of
severance for each year of service.

How to Personally Handle the "Fired" Situation

If you have won any of the previous items, good for you. If you
get to stay on the payroll, act happy, give no word of your status to anyone, and don't "confidentially" tell your co-workers—*none* of them.
Some other tips:

1. No guilt! Most dismissals are due to personality conflicts, which are not only avoidable, but common, well-
known no-fault problems that can crop up anywhere. It
may be a lousy way to run a conglomerate or step on
someone's career, but it's done every day to the most
competent of employees. So, welcome to the ranks of
those who stuck their necks out!

2. Don't take a vacation. Job finding is a busy, full-time
occupation. Get occupied immediately.

3. No recriminations. You'll need references from that
bum. Anyhow, remember 1: It happens every day.

4. Be prepared to immediately feel anger, shock, guilt, and
depression. It will be a normal reaction to feel those
emotions. Just don't give in to them, too deeply or for
too long. Remember, there *is* a job out there, all you
have to do is to find it!

5. Be prepared to increasingly feel humilation and help-
lessness. You start to feel that you have lost your reason
for being, literally your position in life. No more ritual
of rising early, commuting, coffee breaks, boring meetings, stimulating memo wars, and large-scale projects.

Waves of anger may alternate with clouds of depression. Reminder: there are plenty of jobs out there, and

> If you plan for defeat, that's what will come;
> But if you charge positively into the fray, you can be a winner.

6. Rose-colored Glasses Department: A year or more from now there is an excellent chance that you will look upon this as an opportunity that freed you from a no-win dead end, and permitted you to reexamine yourself, your career, your strengths and accomplishments, and to undoubtedly find a much better position in life. Admit it: when someone else is fired, haven't you sometimes argued whether it was fair or not, and don't you then usually decide it was probably for the best, and that the someone will probably end up with a better job? Go thou and do likewise!

Even if that ideal job doesn't exist out there today, with the proper maneuvering, a job may be invented just to take advantage of your particular strengths. Before you are done, you will not only have a new job, but also a new insight into your strengths, your new-found and well-deserved self-confidence, and the true nature of inner- and job security.

So, let's get to work; there's a lot to be done.

Emergency Procedures

If you are suddenly and officially fired, try to remember—at the very least—the three following rules:

1. Don't lose your temper, don't badmouth the company or your boss, don't start a fight. Play for time, play on their guilt, play for the best terms you can extract.

2. Immediately make plans for continuation of your health insurance coverage. If you can't get it continued, get a nongroup conversion policy, get coverage under your working spouse's contract, or get private nongroup coverage. Many executives forget to do this during the post-firing period, and it could be a very serious mistake.

3. Don't forget to register for unemployment insurance. This is not charity or a moral crime: it is insurance that you or the company have paid the premiums on, and you are entitled to collect on the policy.

Get the Family Involved

1. Yes, get the family involved. Let the spouse and kids know what you are up against, ask for their support, cooperation, and understanding. Warn them it's going to be a strain on everyone. You'll have problems with your short temper, concentration, and love life. You'll be tired and depressed. It will hit you even harder than the death of a close friend.

2. Your spouse will be just as jumpy: part of the time he or she will be a sympathizer, sounding board, hand holder, and keeper of the family ties. The rest of the time your spouse will understandably be mad as hell, frustrated, and extremely apprehensive, blaming you for lost prestige, lost income, and sleepless nights. In short, you'll feel even more guilty, thanks to your spouse.

The remedy is to get everyone, kids and spouse alike, to try and have some perspective on this stressful interlude. It's a chance to pull together, sacrifice together, mature, and learn together. It's an opportunity for a new start and new challenges, and maybe a new career. It's not as bad as having the house burn down or being run over by a car. It's a chance to grow, together. So, let your spouse read this section right now: you both have a job to do!

3. Make a budget, see how you'll hold up financially if you don't get a job for, say, six months. Let the kids know if it means no new motorcycle; they're part of the family, too. Talk to your car finance company and home mortgage company if you see trouble ahead. They can work with you, if you give them some advance warning.

4. Don't withdraw from your social life, continue your contacts with neighbors and friends. Keep active in your hobbies, but remember that finding a job is a full-time job, so don't neglect it.

5. Keep your campaign going on a regular basis. Don't sleep in! Don't waste time! Put in 40 hours per week on job finding. Get an office set up someplace. Have a plan for the whole day, just as you did at the office.

6. Don't take a job on the rebound, just to show the guys at the old office a thing or two. It usually is a big mistake, if you haven't really thought through where you want to go, what you want to do, and what will really make you happy on a lifetime basis.

    Maybe you now have new goals, or maybe you learned something about yourself as a result of your recent harrowing experience? Perhaps you want a job with less pressure, or more responsibility, or less risk? This is an ideal time to reexamine yourself. (For more on this, see Chapter 19.)

Look on this as a vital learning experience, a part of growing: you can emerge from this battle somewhat bruised, but a much wiser, more mature and realistic human being.

Early Warning Fire Detection

The last chapter will give you the rules on "fire prevention." It consists of not getting fired by doing a good job, keeping your eyes and ears open, and keeping the communication channels open with your boss. This advice will also give you some early-warning "fire detection," or advance warning capability.

Here is some additional advice that I hope will give you time to prepare for a possible termination.

1. The most obvious clue is a change (for the bad) in your boss's personal attitude towards you. All bosses have occasional bad days, when they may forget to say "good morning." Problems at home or with the boss's own boss can sour an otherwise cheery disposition. But when you are the only one who starts to get the "treatment" a red flag should go up in your mind. Quickly arrange a personal meeting with the boss, and explain that you have received some signals that may indicate a problem, and you wish to help solve the problem, not be part of it. The boss may or may not be open with you, but it's worth a shot to try this anyhow.

2. If the above doesn't work out, watch for the deadly second phase: you are not invited to key meetings, not copied on office memos, and your advice or expertise is no longer sought.

   Stop any thoughts of "it's only my imagination," or "he really doesn't mean it," or "this will blow over—I'm doing a great job." It is not your imagination—he does mean it, and it won't blow over. Great job or not, the boss in his infinite wisdom has decided that you and he are not compatible. Get your job-search program started in earnest at this point: be prepared!

   You can also try other escape hatches and ploys:

talking with your mentor or sponsor (if you have developed or found one), or quietly investigating an internal transfer to another job. But face it: if the boss won't level with you, and continues the "treatment," your days are numbered on your present job.

3. This final area of early-detection has little to do with your boss, and a lot to do with you, your company, and industry. It is not a specific warning, but rather a generalized set of clues that could possibly lead to a "fire" in the future, or at least some career stumbling blocks.

> You have no "sponsors." You have been on the same job for many years. Your pay hasn't kept pace with your peers'. You've been passed over for promotion. Your job seems useless, undemanding, a dead end. You are having a personality clash with someone on the right team. You are on the wrong team. You are constantly involved in memo wars.

> Your company is in financial trouble. It's in a dying industry. Your company may be sold, merged, or reorganized. In a merger, your company would likely be the "buyee" and not the buyer. In the event of such a merger, you suddenly find yourself as a long-term, highly paid employee whose function is duplicated in the buyer company. The buyer says, "There will be no changes in management." But of course you know better.

If any of these apply to you, you should probably make definite plans to leave in any case. It doesn't sound like you have much of an attractive future if you stay. And perhaps, no future at all.

SEVEN

THE ADVANTAGES OF BEING A KNOWN QUANTITY

T he most-used company tactics, as we now know, all involve personal knowledge or contact:

1. Promote underling.
2. Promote from other department.
3. Personal contact/referral/approach a known candidate.
4. Spread word to friends in the trade.
5. Hire a recruiter.

A company hires a recruiter so that he will personally review and screen the leading candidates. The recruiter attempts to find known, respected people not on the market, who are gainfully employed, and not those faceless, unknown people who already wrote to the company.

At the lower management levels, the hirer may settle for less-efficient screening:

6. A recommended candidate from an employment agency.

And what do you think that leaves as the company tactics least trusted or used? The answer is, of course, the most impersonal approaches. These most uncertain and "unknown" ways are:

7. Run a company ad for a few of the open jobs and get answers from hundreds of strangers.
8. Read incoming resumes—more hundreds of strangers.
9. Read old resumes that Personnel has saved. ("These people are probably back to work already if they were any good.")
10. Maybe answer someone's "position wanted" ad. ("This guy is desperate—maybe we can get him cheap.")

What a coincidence, you might say, that those nonpersonal techniques least-favored by companies are the most favored approaches of the shy, rejected, easily hurt job searcher who sends out hundreds of cold Dear Sir resumes to companies, dozens of resumes in answer to ads, and perhaps considers running his own ads, too.

Our same forlorn job searcher usually is tempted to extend these nonpersonal and low-priority techniques, and also carries out blanket-mailings to agencies and recruiters. His resume comes flying over the transom, along with 50 or 500 others each day; they will probably never be referred to again by anyone.

Examples of Successful Known Quantities

In the meantime, dozens of other, happier scenes are taking place every day.

> "Congratulations, *Son,* you are certainly following in my footsteps." (How's that for a known-quantity decision?)
> Good luck, John, now that Kurt was hit by a truck, you will just step up and take his place! You were already *doing* most of his job anyway."
> "This is a great opportunity for you, Rosemary, to transfer out of corporate staff accounting into the divisional offices and get some real-world, hands-on experience. *They know all about you,* and know you'll do the job."
> "Welcome aboard, Jack. The agency people have been *telling me* how great your work is—creative and all that—and we sure need a VP of creativity, so here's your new office."
> "Well, Jerry, you sure were hard to find. We needed the world's leading left-handed reactologist, and it took Bruce Wayne and Associates five months to *headhunt* you for us. Glad you finally relented and decided to join us."

The moral of all this is: Become a Known Quantity.

Why You Are Not Known

You probably have real reasons to be despondent, to be in the depths of despair: How could *you* ever become "known"?

1. If there was an easy way, you'd have thought it up already, right? Right.

2. You also had the bad luck to be born with only one mother and one father, and neither of them a millionaire.

3. You made it through college with no one knowing your name—not the profs, students, coaches, or bartenders. It wasn't your fault: you did work your way through, so you didn't have time to be a politician or a BMOC (Big Man On Campus).

4. Your college roommates were totally unlike those of Slow Jim, the campus idiot (bottom of the class). His roommates all had fathers who were corporate presidents, influential congressmen, or entrepreneurs who like to bring in young people as future executives. Your own roomie's parents were a mixed bag. A three-time loser on parole from prison for extortion, a starving musician on dope, an alcoholic life insurance salesman, and a nervous widow pushing Sonny through 'ole' Dad's school. You know, it *does* sound like your kind of luck.

    Maybe you're right: it's tough to become a Known Quantity to those in the know.

5. And today, who do you know?

    The gumchewing bowling-shoe lady.

    Your hot-tempered and self-serving boss.

    Your nagging wife or foul-mouthed husband.

    The selfish landlord.

    Your senile uncle.

    And your rotten kids, that's who.

It's Time to Become Known

However, it's never too late to develop a circle of contacts who can later help you.

1. Ask your boss if he can help you to develop in your career path. In turn, help him by doing some extra work or report that reflects well on the department.

2. Sign up for a self-improvement course that your personnel department may be offering, on anything from report writing to How to Interview.

3. Send copies of your best office memos far and wide.

4. Wait for an opening about three-quarters of the way into a meeting, and then offer up your splendid idea on how to solve that customer service problem.

5. Write articles for the professional journals in your field.

6. Join some industry associations and professional organizations, and volunteer to become a committee member or chairperson.

7. Arrange to have your job or committee appointments announced in professional and trade publications.

8. Ask people, both inside the company and outside, for advice, information, or help.

9. Keep track of all your friends, acquaintances, business associates, and so on, and keep current on what they are doing and who they know.

That last category includes suppliers and insurance salesmen, lawyers and bankers, business peers and neighbors, lodge members and college alumni. The point is: you do know many people, including "alumni" who previously left the company and went on to another, others who have a second circle of contacts, such as friends at other companies, as well as people you have met at meetings and conventions.

How Not to "Use" Your Friends

Never "use," abuse, or push anyone. In the real world, it doesn't work—not for long. But don't be so shy, or retiring; it is perfectly permissible to allow your friends and business acquaintances to voluntarily decide if they can do you or someone else a favor by passing along your qualifications or availability. Let's put it another way: if a friend of yours were to call you and ask, "Could you give me the name of the manager of Quality Control in your company?," wouldn't you usually tell him? And if he also asked, "What is the best way to inquire about a job in Quality Control in your company?" wouldn't you at the least be flattered that he asked for your advice? And if you and he had lunch one day, and he sold you on his qualifications, wouldn't you help him *and* the company by mentioning his name to the Q.C. manager?

Likewise, if he was not right for the job or the company, wouldn't you be helping him by explaining the facts to him? And if he ends up at a competitor, and two years later *you* need a similar favor from him, wouldn't you feel relieved that you originally treated him right?

Becoming a known quantity is an important part of successful job-finding, and so is knowing how to take advantage of being known. *Not* to take advantage of people, but to capitalize on the fact that known people do get the jobs. You need to use all of your contacts, old and new, near and far. We're going to show you how, systematically, in the following chapter.

THE CONTACT TRAIL

t's time to address the basic problem of trying to develop contacts. As a reminder: Chapter 4 gave you your 15 Job-Hunting Strategies, to be utilized in the same priority-order as listed there. The first 10 strategies are quite useful. In addition, they also serve as a warmup for important strategy 11: *Select target companies—get contacts inside.*

Introduction: Contacts and Target Companies

Your first-level contacts are people you know personally: past bosses, fellow workers, family and friends, salespeople who call on the industry, accountants, trade journal editors, school chums, professors, and so on. They represent the first step in setting up a communications network, and are not usually the people who can hire you directly. This first group is very important, however. They will lead you to that next group—those who are in a position to know of openings or to hire you. Your second tier consists of all your first-level referrals, hopefully inside your target companies.

Now, it's time to be some writing, to ensure you are fully prepared.

Your Written Contact Preparations

1. Set up a card file of all potential first-level contacts. Make a note when you do make contact. Further update the file with their second-tier referrals. Thus, this file will contain the names of first-level contacts plus the names they feed you.
2. Set up a separate card file of each second-tier name, together with a notation of who gave you their name.
3. Make your list of your target companies.

4. Make up a checklist of what you intend to discuss with your contacts, to make sure that:

    (a) They'll know what type of *job* you are looking for.

    (b) They'll know which *companies* you are particularly interested in.

    (c) You'll remember to ask them for executives' names *they* would be willing to call themselves on your behalf.

    (d) You'll ask for names of executives you might contact *directly* and be permitted to mention the name of the referring person.

    (e) You'll have needed information on the executive being called, the target company, its problems and opportunities.

    (f) You'll have a written record of advice on how to best approach the company.

5. For your prime target companies, get as much additional background as possible. Visit their offices and ask for an annual report, talk with friends and former employees; also, be sure to look up their financial and other data in the business or stock market reference department of your local library.

6. From all your sources, accumulate a written record of the contributions you might make to each of the targets. You'll want to lace these into your contact conversations as a means of demonstrating your interest and capability in solving the target company's problems.

Once you have completed these preparations, you will be ready to start utilizing your contacts.

Making Contact

Your first-level contacts will come in differing degrees of friendship or closeness, ranging from a blood relative to a friend, a business acquaintance, or perhaps someone you met at a convention last year. In each case, the basic rules are the same: relax, flatter them, and remember that everyone likes to give advice.

Talk as if the contact were an old friend you have known for years:

1. "How great it is to see/talk to/reestablish contact with you."
2. "I plan on looking for a greater career challenge and I need your advice on my goals and plans."
3. "I specifically need some information on the _____, _____, and _____ companies. They are my targets as of today."
4. "You have a lot of friends in the industry—I need some names of high-level people in these target companies. Can you help? Can I call or write them, or—could you?"
5. "You know what's going on in the industry; what other companies in my area may need help with . . ."
6. "Would you know of any companies now having a management reorganization?"

As an alternate script for saying all of this, see item 4 in the following section.

Striking the Correct Tone

1. Approach your first-level contacts on a low-key, friendly, non-pressure basis. You can relax and so can they: you will not be asking them for a job.

2. That is, when you make your first-level contacts, you'll just be asking them for some advice.

3. You won't have to ask them to do anything, except to listen. Don't press them to accept 10 copies of your resume (but you should offer, in a low-key manner, to send them one). If they volunteer for copies, send them of course, particularly if they have someone in mind whom they will be seeing soon and might want to present with a copy.

4. People like to help, and you *are* asking for their advice. If handled right, they will be flattered by your request. Here's another sample script on what you ask after first saying, "How great it is to see you again":

   (a) "I need your advice on a personal marketing campaign."

   (b) "Looking ahead, there are few, if any, opportunities for me at ABCD Corporation" (and/or) "I need to make a job move to a faster-moving company" (and/or) "How can I get into pharmaceuticals?" (and/or) "I need to make more money now, because of _____."

   (c) "Do you have any marketing advice or suggestions?"

   (d) "I'd like your advice on my goals, too!"

   (e) "I also need to talk to people who are already in the _____ business. Do you have any friends or acquaintances whom I could call, or that you could ask that could give me information on that industry or the _____, _____, _____, _____, and _____ companies? Are there any other companies that may need my expertise, or who may be going through a reorganization?"

   (f) If the answer is "no" to *e*, ask the contact to think about it, and ask if you can call back in three days to see if he has any suggestions, recommendations, or names.

(g)   If this contact is a known good source, instead of offering to call back, ask instead to meet for breakfast, or lunch, or at some convenient 15-minute time slot, and again run through the above questions in person.

How to Prepare

1.   Get a tape recorder, write your own personalized script, and practice the conversation.

2.   Or, practice with your spouse or a friend, on the telephone or in person.

3.   Remember, I can't force you to go through this exercise. But, if you want to duplicate the advice of many outplacement firms in the United States, do what is suggested here. Practice it, and start your contact trail: It will ultimately lead you into becoming that first-in-line candidate, the Known Quantity.

4.   The Final Step in this process is covered in Chapter 15 on "Your Strategy for Target Companies" which outlines how to break through the lines of defense *inside* the target company. In the meantime, rehearse these initial contact approaches. You are purposely being pre-exposed to these techniques, to dramatize early on that you *can* become a Known Quantity to almost any target.

Follow-up and Saying Thank You

1.   After each primary contact, be sure to call the person or write a short thank-you note. You can remind them of

any follow-ups they promised, but the overall tone should be one of appreciation.

2. After each secondary contact, call your primary/referral contact and thank him for the lead. In addition, bounce what you heard off of the primary, to get his reaction and advice on the quality of the secondary contact.

3. Once you are placed successfully, be sure to send a note to all contacts, at the first and secondary levels, thanking them for their efforts and giving some details on your new position.

Our motto is Be Prepared. You never know when you again might have to tap into or completely reactivate your contact trail. Keep it nourished, alive, and well: having a living, communicating network of friends can only help you, in good times or bad.

The Power of Networking

Networking is a leading technique that is now used and taught by many professional outplacement and executive marketing firms. These are the firms that work with corporations or individuals to help find jobs for executives. When performing outplacement for corporations, these firms relieve the corporations of many of the problems that arise when executives are fired, by immediately counseling the executives and helping them to pull together a job search program. As an individual, you can save yourself the trouble and cost, and do it yourself.

Networking is a buzzword of the Eighties; it is simply a broad-scale, wide-angle approach to the targeted or "contact trail" technique given in this chapter. It makes sense to try this technique if you are unable or unwilling to pick your target company or industry at this point in your career. It's like fishing with a very wide net: it's not as targeted, but if you do it diligently, it should turn up a number of interesting leads.

Networking: Summary

First, you round up the names of *all* your contacts: get out your business Christmas card lists, company telephone directories, and so on, and add your old classmates, insurance salespeople, supplier representatives, and the like.

Contact your list, and ask each of them for two to four references or for introductions to other contacts in the business world. (Start with a big list, since succeeding references will be more distant and, therefore, weaker.) Ask *those* contacts for two to four more contacts. Then, do it again with *their* contacts!

Here's the theory: Say you start with 15 personal first-hand (first level) contacts. Each introduces you to three others, for 45 additional contacts. If each of them introduces you to three more, that's 135 additional contacts. If you do it once more, that's 405 more contacts, for a grand total of 600 (including your original 15) contacts.

This technique requires that you:

1. Have some original contacts in the first place.
2. Persevere and get each of them to divulge (or introduce) three contacts to you.
3. Keep careful records of everyone contacted.

It takes courage and commitment on your part to carry this off, plus a rehearsed script asking for "contacts who might know of opportunities in your field." As with the contact trail method, you don't ask for a job, just some contacts. It is an excellent technique for a wide-scale search, and well worth the time and trauma: you are a Known Quantity (to a degree, at least) at each step.

Consultants can explain all this, coach you, and hold your hand. But they charge a fee—and *you* will *still* have to make personal calls. No one else, after all, can do it for you. Moral: Do it yourself and save!

"IT'S WHO YOU KNOW, NOT WHAT YOU KNOW, THAT COUNTS"

SOME CASE STUDIES

F reedom of association is an important right in a democracy. Most of us are free to choose who we want to marry or to socialize with.

But the business office is a different situation. We have little choice when it comes to selecting our boss, co-workers, peers, or most of the other people we are forced to deal with on the job. Thus, we lack control over our interpersonal environment for eight hours each working day, unless, of course, we have the ultimate power to make the hiring and firing decisions. It is this coveted capability that gives a manager some measure of control over his personal environment. So, it's not too surprising that:

People are hired on the basis of their personal compatability with the boss, assuming they can offer a modicum of ability, or at least a hint of "trainability."

People are also fired on the basis of their personality, no matter how much ability they have.

When we consider how valuable, nay, glorious, it is for a manager to be able to control some part of his business interpersonal environment, we can understand and almost forgive the unfair—but 100% true—title of this section.

This fact of business life is highly discriminatory against the disadvantaged in our society: minorities, women, and the poor, along with those other people who:

Are morally incensed at the unfairness of it all.

Are not tuned in to office politics and the need for pull, and are convinced that "if I work hard and keep my nose to the grindstone I'm sure to get ahead."

If you fall into either of these disadvantaged categories, you can ignore these facts of life at your career's peril, or, you can selfishly, greedily, cunningly, and deliberately put them to work for you!

The following examples of pull are not meant to disgust or titillate you; they are true-to-life examples of "How things are out there." You'll also begin to realize that you can retain your personal scruples even while utilizing contacts to get your job.

Case I: The College Grads

The son or two teachers from modest backgrounds was very bright, but he and his parents were among the culturally disadvantaged: they never learned or were taught how to get ahead. They just did not know any better or anyone! As a result, the son worked his way through college as a restaurant dishwasher each summer. That's all he wanted—a job to help meet college expenses. All he got was housework experience at the minimum wage.

His roommate's father was financial vice president for a national manufacturer. The father knew someone in the advertising department, and his son got an exciting part-time job. He worked hard and did a good job. Upon graduation he made up a short resume of his practical experience, together with a list of industry references, and immediately landed a fine job with an advertising agency.

Having learned his who-you-know lesson early in life, the son of the vice president continued to work hard, and also kept his eyes open for further opportunities to become known in his firm and field. His career is now well on its way.

The teachers' son, in the meantime, still has his nose to the grindstone, hoping in his own quiet way that someone, someday, will at last recognize his hard work, talent, and ability.

These young people were equally bright, eager, and talented. But one of them knew the two keys to success in the corporate world: Do a good job and become a Known Quantity. The combination is crucial. Simply doing good work is not always enough to land you a job or to put you on the road to advancement. If you're known, it doesn't matter how good a job you do.

Case II: The Idealist

My daughter Beth (not her real name) is young, bright, and idealistic. She is a free spirit: open, liberal and people-oriented. She categorically rejects the idea that pull should be a factor in the real world, and has always refused to consider any summer jobs in my company.

To digress for a moment, and as a point of contrast, this is the opposite experience of a plant manager that I know.

One of his children was able to get a hard-to-find summer job in his father's company's accounting office, because the father was on speaking terms with the office manager. The father was the Known Quantity in this case, not the child.

His older daughter was offered an attractive full-time position with another leading company in the area. The personnel manager of that second company knew the father: they had once served on a school board together. That helped. As a second fortuitous coincidence, the personnel manager's son also happens to work for the plant manager as a plant supervisor. Thus, the personnel manager had a double reason for hiring my friend's daughter: he knew the plant manager on a civic/personal basis, and it was also an opportunity to help along his *own* son's career in the plant manager's organization. "One hand washes the other," as it is said.

Back to Beth's story: she originally got into an Ivy League school by studying hard and also because her extra-curricular accomplishments resulted in outstanding letters of recommendation. The college felt they had a Known Quantity because of those glowing references, even before they had ever interviewed her. This was pull perhaps, but legitimate and completely self-earned.

As a freshman she worked on the campus newspaper and radio station. With *those* letters of recommendation she then landed a job on her own as a low-paid summer intern on a large newspaper that first summer. For her sophomore year she wanted to earn some money, but well-paying summer jobs had become even harder to find, and she was unable to develop any meaningful leads.

However, I happened to meet a former business acquaintance whom I hadn't seen or talked to in 20 years. We had once worked together for the same company, but had lost touch ever since. We chatted of the good old days, and I mentioned that I was a reader of his wife's articles in the national magazine where she is an assistant editor. I asked if he could find out from his wife how Beth might find a summer job in the communications field, and he suggested that I call his wife directly and ask her.

Please keep in mind: I hadn't seen this man for 20 years, but apparently I was still a somewhat Known Quantity, not a total stranger. I decided to call his wife, whom I had *never* met, identified myself as an old acquaintance of her husband, and modestly bragged about Beth. The wife insisted that Beth send in her clippings and an application, even though there were no known openings available. Beth immediately called her from school, chatted for a while, and got the name of the managing editor to whom she was to direct her application.

Two months then passed and I forgot completely about the incident. Lo and behold, we got a call from the managing editor the very same night as I was polishing up Case I. Beth was asked to start work at an attractive salary the following week.

Note the "long-distance" nature of this remarkable story:

1. This was merely a 20-year-lapsed business acquaintance. (Beth is 19: she wasn't even born when I last saw my friend.)
2. I had never met his wife.
3. His wife had never met Beth, or even heard of her before.
4. The managing editor had never met Beth.

There were two factors that resulted in this success story:

1. Beth did have a terrific, self-earned background: her grades, her clippings, and her prior job experience.

2. But so did many of the 75 other applicants already on file with the magazine. What Beth also had was a tenuous, slender, second-hand, 20-year-old "contact," with all of the original arrangements made by long-distance telephone!

The moral to this story is: ability plus the faintest wisp of a contact can get you a job!

Maybe you are just like Beth: she was disappointed that she had to rely on pull to originally get a job. Her idealism is still strong: she still thinks pull is basically unfair and unjust. But she also knows that she is right for the job, and that her qualifications are first rate. She intends to build her own career and contact trail on her own in the future, and is already working hard at it. Her first article received a by-line, and her editors are very impressed. But those long-distance contacts *did* help put her foot in the door in the first place!

Case III: Four Do-It-Yourself Contact Trails

The cases in this chapter cover all phases of a business career, from college summer jobs on up to senior management positions. This particular case covers a group of four young people, each with a few years of working experience since college graduation.

1. We start with Shelly, a successful music teacher, who has become popular as a performer, teacher, and volunteer coach in various statewide teaching associations, regional competitions, and concerts. Although she is not a gung-ho career climber, she is well known and can get a job in any school system in the state. Shelly is a living example of a do-it-yourself Known Quantity.

2. Shelly's husband works for the government and is well-liked due to his knowledge, enthusiasm, and good personality match. His recent promotions are a result of pull in a sense, but it is based on his known-quantity abilities to: Do the job and work well with the boss, as well as with his co-workers.

3. Susan's career as an engineer is also well on its way, based on her own "operation bootstrap" program. A straight-A student, she is dogged, determined, and persistent in everything she does. As you will see, persistence does pay off. In college she won a number of national awards, writing papers on subjects that she initially knew nothing about, but which she diligently researched and quickly became expert in. Her merits made her a known quantity within her university, and within the ranks of some professional organizations. This led to a summer job offer with a well-known company, and the subsequent offer of a permanent position after graduation. Her resume and work references were so results-oriented that upon graduation she accepted an engineering position with an outstanding firm at an extremely high starting salary.

   She had made herself a Known Quantity, standing out among the throngs of new graduates.

4. Susan's husband is a young research scientist who is similar to the others in this case: he is highly idealistic, completely independent, and abhorrent of any tinge of office political battles or pull. His success is likewise due to a do-it-yourself philosophy: he earned a Ph.D. in his speciality, and proceeded to publish papers and research in his field. He took full advantage of professional journals, seminars, and conferences, presenting his work at meetings around the country. He is now nationally known for his research and publications in his field. He is a Known Quantity in his profession.

Case IV: A Housewife Returns to Work

In a job interview situation, housewives who have returned to work after 20 years of housework and raising children sometimes say: "I worked for three years when I first got married. Now, I'm very, very anxious to rejoin the workforce, but I sometimes feel old, unwanted, and out of touch."

If they do get a job using this approach, it's usually at a very low level, and at a very low wage. They're actually begging for a job—a bad strategy.

There is another way. Consider the case of Helen, who worked as a junior accountant many years before the days of the computer. Twenty years later she mounted a campaign to reenter the workforce.

First, she wrote a short resume. This was unusual, since most housewives in her category don't or can't prepare one.

The resume played up the fact that she set up the books for a small family-owned business, and that she was the treasurer of a number of civic associations.

Some of the major employers in the area interviewed her, but somehow they never had a "suitable" opening. Yet, some attractive 20-year-olds with less experience were hired for the jobs that did become available. Helen's resume got her interviews all right, but that was all.

Helen then took some assignments from a local temporary-help agency, and got some big-company, modern accounting experience in that way. However, as time went by, any new openings went to young girls on the permanent payroll who had full-time seniority; it was time to move on.

Helen then updated her resume with this big-company (albeit temporary) experience and decided to concentrate on looking for a permanent job with a small, rather than large, company. After answering an ad, she became the bookkeeper for a small, struggling firm.

She was quickly promoted to assistant office manager, later had a falling out with the boss, and then answered some ads—this time with a solid, recent, and full-time job entry listed on her resume.

Today Helen is the business office manager in charge of accounting for a small construction company, and has installed new budget controls. She is also going back to school to learn computer programming.

There are a number of morals to this success story:

1. If you hit a brick wall, just go around it if you can't blast through it. No success with large companies? Try a small one—they may be interested in your qualities and offer more opportunity for advancement, besides.
2. If life seems to hand you a lemon, take charge and make it into lemonade. Make up your own script or recipe for success!
3. The only person who can help you (or hold you back) is you! Don't settle for what others want you to do—take the offensive.

Helen discovered that getting ahead, if this is what you want, is an exciting game! Just don't freeze up; play the game as if it *is* a game, and be creative enough to find the winning approach that gets you where you want to go.

Case V: You, Too, Can Be Vice President

This last case is an analysis of the career moves of a Fortune 500 corporate vice president called Bell. He worked most of the time in a hard-charging, quick-changing, profit-squeezed industry; in addition, fickle fate caused him to have some hard bounces along the way. But he enjoyed the challenge and learned to bounce back up again to a higher level.

Bell was recruited right out of a competitive college at graduation. Jobs were tough to find and, as he described it, he was up against a graduating class seemingly full of "serious A students, outgoing campus politicians, and bright, easy-going athletes." Still, the prestigious International Manufacturing Company's campus recruiter found that Bell stood out in two ways.

1. At an unusual 8:30 A.M. pre-interview orientation session on campus, Bell was somewhat nervous but he was the only student who bothered to show up. He was ambitious, and it showed!

2. Bell had very few extra-curricular activities because he was forced to work his way through school. It later developed that the suave interviewer had the same problem when he had gone to school.

Bell's career advanced at the company at a good rate, due to his capability to handle any job, particularly controls and cost reduction. That was the situation for eight years, until a vice president he neither trusted nor admired was promoted to president. At an American Management Association meeting some time later, he met an International "alumnus" who was now the general manager of Moonshine, Inc., a firm in financial trouble. At International, Bell was a known quantity, but he increasingly disliked the cronyism and "Don't Do It Right—Do It By the Book" approach of its new president; so he took the offer of engineering manager from the alumnus at Moonshine, since he was a known quantity to them as well.

The general manager of Moonshine had a political fight with the president a few years later, and lost. Bell updated his resume (just in case), but his cost-reduction contributions outweighed the fact that he had been originally brought in as a member of what was now the wrong team. Nevertheless, the long-term future advancement picture was no longer challenging.

At about this time Bell noticed an article in the trade magazine that covered his depressed industry. He read that the Evermoving Company, coincidentally, also was undergoing a political upheaval. He wrote to their new president, congratulated him, and offered to join his team as an engineering or manufacturing manager. There were no openings, but Bell wrote and called twice more, emphasizing his successes and his practical background. He was surprised to be called in two months later for an interview—for a new manufacturing-control job that was to be created for and tailored to him. Bell's letters had convinced Evermoving that they had a control void in their organization that had been totally unnoticed previously. Bell joined them at a significant increase in salary and responsibility.

A few years later Bell was called by a headhunter and offered the opportunity to get out of staff work and take on a direct-line position as assistant general manager for the Glow Corporation, a medium-sized consumer products company. At last, a line opportunity, and at another large increase in salary. This fit his career plans for broader line responsibility in a more modern and expansive industry, and he accepted the position.

Ten years later, after good progress career-wise, the fickle finger of fate finally hit: the Glow Company was sold, disbanded, and only the patents and trademarks were brought into the new owner's business and added to his own, similar line of items. It was going to be D.C.M. for everyone from the president to the porters. (D.C.M.: Don't Come Monday.)

But Bell was prepared. Out went the resumes, back came an offer to be general manager of Laughing Stock, a small company in his old depressed industry. It was a risky situation: the owners were new to the industry, the company was losing money and for six months had unsuccessfully been on the block to be sold to the highest bidder. Bell saw the D.C.M. at his old company was but a few months away, there were no other challenging offers around, unemployment was not really an option—so he decided to take the offer on an interim basis. Two years later the company was *still* about to be sold: it was now making a good profit, but the E.P.A. was after them on almost a weekly basis. Bell argued with the Board of Directors to build a new, modern, and environmentally sound plant in the Sun Belt where the customers were all fleeing, but was turned down.

Bell went with a leader (20 times larger) in the consumer products industry, doing what he does so well: building an organization as Vice President of Operations, and saving big dollars. He ultimately got the job because of the many friends he had in the industry and in key supplier companies; his references were all A-1.

There are a number of morals to this story:

1. If you want to succeed, have a plan on how you intend to get there.

2. Don't settle just because you are sidetracked, for example, into the Personnel Department. If you want to be in Operations, go for it! If not in your present company, seek your life's work elsewhere. Don't trade your life's challenge for so-called security! Life is too short.

3. Don't let temporary setbacks set you back! Everyone has them at one time or another. Bell had his share along the way, but his vice-presidential salary, profit sharing, bonuses, and inner feelings of accomplishment and success tend to cushion and ameliorate all those blows.

4. However, if you unswervingly aspire to be the president and nothing less will do, there are two things you should avoid: being in the wrong specialty, and too much job hopping. Bell was not a marketing man, and that is a definite prerequisite for the presidency at his current company. Most presidents come out of marketing, sales, or finance. Also, from a presidential standpoint, Bell's record of six companies is against him on a statistical basis. Some surveys show that most presidents have had only one, two or three company associations. So don't jump around precipitously if you seriously intend to become president of your present firm.

    On the other hand, the pyramid quickly gets smaller

at the *very* top, and if you seek real challenge, you may have to find it outside in another pyramid (or even in your *own* business with yourself at the very top).

Finally, we should note the five different vehicles Bell successfully used when he decided to move.

1. His extra-effort points earned at the college recruiting session;
2. That company "alumni" that hired him;
3. Writing to a newly-appointed president;
4. Being known to be a headhunter; and
5. Having friends in the industry.

Each one meshed—it was a case of using the right strategy at the right time at the right place. And each is a variation on being known or making yourself known. It is, after all, a matter of who you know if you want to get ahead.

We have now reached the point where it is time to start *your* job-finding campaign. First, we will help you develop convincing, can't-miss letters and resumes (see Chapter 10).

Next, we'll cover writing to companies; mailings to search firms, answering ads, and contacting employment agencies; and your strategy for target companies.

Finally, come the chapters on interviewing, negotiating, and some closing tips and suggestions.

T E N

WRITING YOUR LETTERS AND RESUMES

There you sit, frustrated, uncomfortable, and alone in your chair, trying to write a warm, friendly, and impressive letter to a company executive you have never met, asking him to meet with you and hopefully to hire you. Your palms begin to get sweaty and stiff; you feel the insidious pangs of writer's cramp overtaking your digits; and soon you find yourself consumed by a full-blown case of writer's block: the words-stop-coming disease.

You try your hand at writing the world's most impressive resume and you end up twitching and staring at what you have written. You realize that you've merely scribbled words on some paper—and the words are anything but a living, dynamic, in-person portrait of the real you. Back you go to letter writing: this time in answer to an ad or to draft a letter to headhunters. But all you can think of is: "They will get 1,000 letters. What can I say that really stands out?"

You are in need of help: a plan of attack, some overall guidance, and some examples of successful letters and resumes. Fear not—this chapter will make it all very easy for you.

Before we start attacking, you must first remember that a letter or resume has only one real purpose: to get you an interview. It's not your life story, it's a piece of attractive bait! Here's how to do it.

The Easy Way to Write Your Resume

1. Go back to the earlier lists we asked (nay, insisted) that you draw up: the projects you are most proud of, their order of priority, and the self-analysis questions on your career interests and goals.

2. Write down the resume heading. That's easy: name, address, and phone number!

3. Write out in a short paragraph (1 to 4 sentences) your

Objective, the next item on your resume. See the lists you compiled for your basic career objective. Example: "A demanding position in marketing with a consumer products company . . ."

If you have two objectives, it's usually best to write two separate resumes. Just be clear in your mind what your objective is for each resume.

4. Next on the resume itself comes a summary paragraph; it might be combined with the objective. Don't write it yet, however. Wait until the resume is completed, and then come back and summarize who you are and what you can do.

For example: "over ten years of successful experiences in the sale of . . . broad experience in launching new products . . ."

5. Now you have two format choices. (I told you this was going to be easy!) Select one of the following:

Chronological Resume: List the dates, company name, your title and two to five accomplishments for each job you have held, starting with the present and then going back in time. Your later jobs must have the most accomplishments. Remember to use the dramatic action words we discussed when you first made up your accomplishment list. This chronological layout is the standard format for most job searchers.

Functional Resume: This format concentrates on and accentuates the types of functions you can perform. Almost as an afterthought, it also lists in a condensed form the dates and companies, again in reverse chronological order. If the latter list of employers is too long or is otherwise a negative factor, consider leaving it out completely.

This functional format is recommended when you want to play down the fact that you:

(a) Worked for 27 different companies

(b) Worked for only six companies, but over a period of only three years, averaging out to six months for each "job-hopping" experience.

(c) Are 40, 50, or 60 years old, and don't want to accentuate the ancient dates of your early jobs.

(d) Worked for some companies whose rotten reputation would reflect poorly on you.

(e) Have recently changed your career field after 25 years, so that your new field's experience only totals six months.

6. Resume Writing Guidelines:

(a) Don't get too personal: no one usually cares that you garden, or collect rocks, or like to fish. Give personal and educational information at the very end, unless education is important in your field, or you are a recent college graduate.

(b) Other personal no-no's: no references to age, sex, marital status, or religion. No photo, either.

(c) Give no salary information or names of references.

(d) *Do not* tell your every wonderful deed! Save a few impressive stories for the interview.

(e) Accentuate the positive! If you have little or no education, emphasize any and all experience. If you are old, accent your seasoned judgment and maturity.

(f) Specific accomplishments *must always* be listed— give savings or sales increases and the like, in *dollars, percents*.

Reminder: A resume will help you to see the real you.

Read it and see how great you really are!

Use it to help structure your interviews.

But remember, it's just a piece of bait, meant to interest, intrigue, and snare you an interview: it can never get you a job.

How to Write Your Letters

1. Here are some general reminders that apply to letters and resumes: Use high-rag content paper, get a neat and clear printing job, don't update or correct with pen or pencil. Type it, neatly.

2. In your letters, as in your resume, don't get too personal, normally give no salary information, accentuate the positive.

3. Another "Don't" for letters or resumes: don't hire someone to write a super-slick version. These are obviously ghost-written and you lose your credibility.

4. You need three basic letters: writing to (A) headhunters; (B) companies; and (C) answering ads. Samples are given at the end of this chapter.

    (a) *Headhunters:*

    Two paragraphs are usually sufficient.

    Attach a resume.

    In an early mailing, run a test to see if giving your salary helps or hurts the response. Headhunters do need to know this information early in the game.

    Any time response is poor, completely re-do your letter and/or resume before your next mailing.

    Also plan to send a follow-up letter after a while if no positive response is received; make it different, too.

(b) *Companies:*

In writing a letter to a company, the most important rule to remember is: Be a Known Quantity. At first, you will be mailing standardized letters to strange executives you never met in companies you have only vaguely heard of. (A resume in a letter format is more personal—see the examples in this chapter.) With a lot of luck, you may get a job this way—but don't count on it.

Such mailings are actually most useful as a test, a warm-up, a refining and learning stage in preparation for Strategy 11: become a known quantity to a key hirer in the target company, and then call him—don't write.

If a letter is needed for any other reason (Thank You, etc.) you should no longer have a case of writer's block. You will then be writing to someone you know about, who also knows of you; perhaps you two have already met.

(c) *Answering Ads:*

Read the ad and pretend *you* wrote it. Then try to guess what response you would look for. Most likely, this will be a cover letter with specific references to how you fit the specific requirements outlined in the ad. Tailor your response to each ad.

Letters—Summary

Resumes are general, so make your letters as specific and personal as you can.

No life stories; no one has the time (or interest) to real all about you. Try to get to Strategy 11 quickly, so that letter-writing can become your personal voice, not a college thesis or an anonymous form letter.

Important Warnings.   Your letter and resume will receive only about five or ten seconds of attention, so:

1.   No typographic errors in your letter or resume. No spelling errors or type-overs either! These are automatic causes for your materials to be filed in the wastebasket.

2.   With only five to ten seconds, you must grab the reader's immediate attention: A strong summary in your resume; a sure opening paragraph in your letter; and a careful printing and layout job as well.

It's Time for Some Examples

The remainder of this chapter is devoted to letters and sample resumes for the job hunter who seeks to project style and executive-level knowhow.

(Address)

(Date)

Ms. Joan Klugman
Mouthspray Distillers Company
1375 Park Avenue
New York, New York   10001

Dear Joan:

It was great talking to you today. It sounds like you and Mouths-pray Corporation were meant for each other.

As we discussed, I have a problem—there is little challenge in the P.C.P. Company and no opportunity for further professional growth.

On a confidential basis I'd like to explore other companies in order to more fully apply my hands-on experience in marketing management.

If you have any further suggestions or leads in our industry, please give me a call. I'm delighted that you plan to see Mr. Dan Grammer and, in passing, tell him of my qualifications.

Again, best regards to you and your family. Let's have lunch again soon.

Sincerely,

(Signature)
(Typed Name)

Follow-Up Letter To First-Level Contact. This letter is general enough to be adapted to almost any functional area of responsibility.

(Address)

(Date)

Mr. Hickory Dock
President
Crocus Corporation
1684 Third Avenue
New York, New York   10019

Dear Mr. Dock:

Sam Truncate suggested at lunch today that I send you a copy of my resume for your review. Sam indicated that you and he had discussed your long-term staffing needs, and that my name came up. I'm happy to have this opportunity to share my background with you.

As Sam probably mentioned, I would be most interested if Crocus had an available, demanding position with broad manufacturing management responsibilities. A review of my enclosed resume will reveal that I can offer Crocus over 15 years of results-oriented plant experience. I have been involved in a broad range of troubleshooting and problem-solving activities in a multiplant operation. My greatest areas of achievement stem from my ability to develop and initiate significant cost reduction and productivity improvement programs. I also offer an excellent supporting educational background with an MBA degree in business administration augmenting an undergraduate degree in industrial engineering.

At any rate, Sam is confident that I have a great deal to offer Crocus in contributing to increased productivity, cost reductions, and overall efficiency. I would be pleased to meet with you in the near future to further explore any opportunities.

Sincerely yours,

(Signature)
(Typed Name)

Enclosure

Targeted Cover Letter To "Referred Contact"

(Address and Phone Number)

(Date)

Mr. Richard Gotrocks
Vice President of Operations
Big Max Company
16 North Place
Mount Holly, California   90028

Dear Mr. Gotrocks:

I noted with great interest your intention to replace your Thorne facility with a new plant in Ford, South Carolina.

I have extensive experience in the successful planning and execution of such a move:

At Massters & Johnson, I coordinated the move and startup of the Products Plant into a new modern facility—on time and within budget.

At Glamor Products Corporation, I consolidated the Los Angeles plant operations into the New Jersey headquarters site, for an ongoing savings of $200,000 per year.

Last weekend, I was discussing these projects with Oscar Peterson, a long-time mutual friend, and he immediately suggested that I share this information with you.

I am currently Vice President of Engineering for a Fortune 500 company, and would consider an unusual opportunity to more fully challenge my capabilities.

Please give me a call if you are interested. Oscar, by the way, sends his best personal regards.

Sincerely,

(Signature)
(Typed Name)

Targeted Letter to Referred Contact. Unless you have a knock-out and directly applicable resume, do not include it with such a first letter.

(Letterhead)

(Date)

(Address)

Dear Ms. Blank:

Based on your corporate growth record, your organization may be interested in my experience and contributions. As a successful (financial) executive, I now seek an opportunity to apply my general management expertise to a more growth-oriented organization.

I am currently Financial Vice President of a Fortune 500 company where my accomplishments include:

Operating costs cut by over $4 million through cost control and 35% higher productivity.

Inventory investment decreased by over $3 million.

Backorders reduced by 35%.

Profit margins and ROI at an all-time high.

The attached record of career growth and contributions to profit could be of immediate interest. If you would like to discuss these qualifications in greater detail, I will be happy to do so at your convenience.

Sincerely,

(Signature)
(Typed Name)

Cover Letter to a Company or Headhunter. If mailed to a headhunter, start this with: "Based on the outstanding record of your corporate clients, . . ." This type of letter could also be used by a manufacturing/operations/distribution executive.

(Address)

(Date)

ABC Company
123 Fourth Avenue
New York, New York   10018

Attention: Mr. Albert Brooks
            Vice President, Operations

Dear Mr. Brooks:

I am currently employed as a personnel manager for DEF Corporation, and seek a position of greater challenge and career potential. Recognizing that it may be considered somewhat unusual to
leave a relatively stable environment during these unstable times, I
am nonetheless hopeful that (your organization)* is in need of additional professional, hands-on management.

Areas in which I can have major positive impacts are cost control
and profitability, organization building, and personnel motivation.

Attached please find a copy of my resume; if, after receiving it, you
feel it to be mutually beneficial, I would appreciate the opportunity
to meet with you.

Respectfully,

(Signature)
(Typed Name)

---

*Broadcast Cover Letter to Companies or Search Firms. This letter is general
enough to be adapted to many different functional areas.*
** If writing to a search firm or college alumni placement office, substitute the fol-
lowing: "... you may have a current client that ..."*

(Address)

(Date)

Mr. Don Evans
President
Franco-Germain Company
456 Second Avenue
New York, New York   10011

Dear Mr. Evans:

Based on research for opportunities that would permit a greater challenge of my management skills, your organization has come to my attention as one that could be interested in my background and experience.

I am seeking a demanding position with broad (Sales Management) responsibilities. A review of my enclosed resume will reveal that I offer over 10 years of field management experience. I have been involved in a wide range of troubleshooting and problem-solving activities. My greatest areas of achievement stem from my ability to develop and initiate significant motivation and salesforce productivity improvement programs. I also offer an excellent supporting educational background with an MBA degree in Business Administration, augmenting my undergraduate degree in Marketing.

Confident that I have a great deal to offer in contributing to increased sales, I would be pleased to meet with you in the near future.

Sincerely yours,

(Signature)
(Typed Name)

Enclosure

Broadcast Cover Letter to Companies or Search Firms. This letter is general enough to be adapted to almost any functional area of responsibility.

(Printed Letterhead or Typewritten Address)

(Date)

Mr. Robert Hope
Vice President of Personnel
Warner Chemicals
P.O. Box 1868
Parkersburg, Virginia   26106

Dear Mr. Hope:

Thank you for your recent phone call. Because of my continued interest in your firm, and the fact I feel strongly that I can make an important management contribution, I was delighted to receive your positive response to my letter.

I'm a marketing and sales executive with a consistent record of success, highly goal oriented, with hands-on experience in the chemical industry. I have the ability to get results through a low-key, we-can-do-it approach that defuses aggression and effectively and enthusiastically builds commitment and teamwork. The enclosed resume provides some highlights.

Production oriented, I can "produce" sales, profits, good organization, and successful follow-through. As an experienced executive, I also offer analytical talent, and sound business judgment. I am free to relocate or travel to enhance my career.

Please thank Mr. Garvey for his interest; I can assure you both that my experience can be applied immediately and profitably to your operations. Can we discuss this in person sometime?

Cordially,

(Signature)
(Typed Name)

Response Letter to Interested Company. This letter is general enough to be adapted to many different functional areas.

(Printed Letterhead—Name, Address, Phone Number)

(Date)

Mr. Ed Franklin, President
M.N.O. Company
123 Third Avenue
New York, New York   10019

Dear Mr. Franklin:

Are you satisfied with your traffic and distribution costs? . . . your human resource/industrial relations progress? . . . your plant management? If some of these areas require improvement, I would appreciate the opportunity of discussing how my capabilities can be profitable to your company. My management techniques have been developed and refined during a progression of positions in manufacturing, distribution, personnel, and administrative services in two Fortune 500 companies. In addition, I have a BS in Business from Brown University.

My responsibilities have included the development of organization and operating plans, budgets (operating and capital), the establishment of cost reduction methods, and the complete accountability for the profit and loss status of the operation. These responsibilities included the development of procedures to attain performance goals for day-to-day operations, and for ensuring long-term contributions to profitability and growth.

I am an accomplished executive with the drive and personality to get the job done.

The enclosed resume will provide additional background information for your consideration. I would welcome the opportunity of meeting you and discussing how my experience and skills might be applicable and beneficial to your organization. I believe that my background can be an asset to the future growth and profitability of the M.N.O. Company. May we discuss this at your earliest convenience?

Sincerely,

(Signature)
(Typed Name)

Enclosure

Broadcast Cover Letter to Companies.

(Printed Letterhead or Typewritten Address)

(Date)

Mr. David N. Goliath
President
Fiddle Chemical Company
1354 Old Post Road
Grace, Maryland   21098

Dear Mr. Goliath:

Thank you for your time and consideration during my visit yester-day. I enjoyed meeting you and learning more about your com-pany—its problems, opportunities, managerial style, and philoso-phy.

As we discussed, my background, experience, and success have been in the areas that could be of interest to you, particularly my turnaround expertise in the (operating) areas. I also sense a shared compatability in the outlook and managerial approach of Fiddle Chemical Company, yourself, and my own approach.

I am enthusiastic about the future of your company, and would welcome the opportunity to discuss this further.

Thank you again. I am hopeful that we can talk some more.

Sincerely,

(Signature)
(Typed Name)

/ns

Thank You Letter After Interview. This letter can be adapted to a number of different functional areas.

(Address)

(Date)

Mrs. Fran Field
Tolyer Brothers Company
(Address)

Dear Mrs. Field:

Thank you for your time last Wednesday. I enjoyed our discussion and learned a great deal during the tour you arranged for me, which Jim Hardly conducted. Jim was very helpful and I would appreciate your thanking him on my behalf.

As we agreed, my related (systems) experience should be of great help on your new _____ project.

I am very interested in a position with Tolyer Brothers Company, and look forward to hearing from you.

Sincerely yours,

(Signature)
(Typed Name)

Thank You Letter After Interview. This letter can be adapted to a number of different functional areas.

(Address)

(Date)

Mr. John Y. Smith, Director
Keylock Associates
270 Park Avenue
New York, New York   10017

Dear Mr. Smith:

It was a pleasure meeting with you and discussing the opportunities that the consulting profession can offer to men with my background. The advantages are certainly strong—the opportunities to learn, to contribute, and to grow.

I was quite attracted by these advantages, but was also interested in other channels for my energies and interests. As you may recall, I would also like to actively participate and implement; that is, to work into line activities, as opposed to staff. In view of my interest in both planning *and* actively directing, I'm sure it is in our joint best interest that I inform you that I have decided not to choose consulting as a lifetime career.

May I extend my sincere appreciation and thanks to Joe Tully, Ralph Shelley, and yourself, for your courteous and thoroughly professional background information on the consulting profession. If in the future I am ever in the position to be of service to you or your company, please be assured that your past courtesies will not be forgotten.

Although I recognize that you do not engage in executive recruiting, I would appreciate your holding on to my file and resume, in case a client should ever require someone with my particular background and skills.

Thank you again for your time and consideration.

Very truly yours,

(Signature)
(Typed Name)

jc

Thanks But No Thanks Letter After Interview.

(Address)

(Date)

(Address)

Gentlemen:

I am responding to your search for a capable and experienced plant manager. This letter is to summarize my background and its relevance to your requirements for this position.

For the last 10 years, I have worked for Cornpone Products Corporation. When I joined them, after graduating from State University, I became an engineer with complete process and quality control responsibility. This included handling customer relations in the field.

My progression proceeded rapidly through various levels of production supervision culminating as the Plant Manager. During my advancement, I became the corporate expert in various specialty products, and the manufacturing liaison between Marketing and R&D in product development.

The last three years as Plant Manager have provided the opportunity to use my problem-solving ability, motivational techniques, and organizational talents to achieve corporate goals.

Some of my personal accomplishments include:

A yearly energy savings of $200,000 with a capital investment of $60,000.

Negotiated two successful union contracts.

Developed and implemented maintenance, personnel, and production planning systems.

Enclosed is my resume, which gives a more comprehensive summary of my experience and accomplishments. Realizing that it is difficult to communicate thoroughly in writing how I can benefit your company, I look forward to the opportunity to speak to you personally.

Sincerely,

(Signature)
(Typed Name)

Enclosure

Cover Letter—Answering Ad.

(Personal Letterhead)

(Date)

(Address)

Gentlemen:

As Vice President of Manufacturing for a company doing $150 million annual sales, I cut material yield losses in half, adding $210,000 to profits in my first year.

My professional history includes achievements in manufacturing management, cost control, and labor relations.

Here are some of the things I have done.

Cut process rejects by $190,000 per year.

Earlier (for another company) I reduced operating expenses by 10% ($260,000) per year in four succeeding years.

Introduced industrial engineering and applied work standards to manufacturing operations.

Initiated manual cost system in branch plant leading the way to improved contribution from 20% to 35%.

Participated in three union contract negotiations and administered grievance procedure.

My formal education includes a Master of Science in Management degree from Cornell College.

I would be happy to give you more information at a personal interview.

Very truly yours,

(Signature)
(Typed Name)

A Letter-Answer to an Ad—With No Resume Attached.

(Address)

(Date)

Box B-2468
New York Times
229 West 43 Street
New York, New York   10036

Dear Sir:

In response to your advertisement for an Administrative Assistant, I am enclosing a copy of my resume for your consideration.

As you will note from my resume, I will graduate from Queens College in June with a major in Psychology and a minor in Sociology. The research and analytical skills I have developed would be valuable assets for the position you describe. Both my written and verbal communication skills are excellent.

While working to help finance my education, I have been promoted to positions of greater responsibility and leadership. As part of a class requirement, I designed a survey of randomly selected courses to determine the extent to which local indsutry information is presented. The faculty and student questionnaires were specifically developed for this study. I analyzed responses and published a report on my findings, which was circulated to the local chamber of commerce.

I would appreciate the opportunity to meet with you and look forward to your favorable reply.

Sincerely,

(Signature)
(Typed Name)

Enclosure

Cover Letter Answering Ad—College Undergraduate.

(Address)

(Date)

Box F392
Times
New York, New York   10108

Dear Madam/Sir:

This is in response to your ad for a Senior Engineering Executive.

My background is a very close fit to your criteria. Specifically, I am a trained mechanical engineer and a production and inventory control expert, with multinational experience in blue-ribbon corporations, covering both consumer and industrial products. My judgment has been honed most recently as Chief Engineer for a multithousand employee manufacturing group.

I am, most importantly, a highly sophisticated and pragmatic executive, with a solid approach to management, organization, and cost/profit solutions.

If you are interested, I will be happy to provide you with additional information.

Sincerely,

(Signature)
George Hamilton

Enclosure

Cover Letter—Answering Ad.

(Address)

(Date)

7870 Times
New York, New York   10108

Dear Sir:

My proven strength in the (toy industry)* is in improving productivity—and bottom-line profits. Recent accomplishments include:

Operating costs cut by over $4 million, through less waste and
25% higher productivity of equipment and workforce.

Profit margins now at all-time high.

Inventory investment decreased by over three million dollars
with a simultaneous 35% reduction in back orders.

I know that I can help you to build a productive organization
strongly committed to low costs, improved profits, and successful
growth.

After reading your ad, I am convinced that my qualifications should
be of interest to you, and I look forward to hearing from you soon.

Sincerely,

(Signature)
Hartley Davison

Enclosure

Cover Letter—Answering Ad.
* Or any other industry, as well.

(Your Address)

(Date)

Mr. Morgan Beatty
Chairman of the Board
Mako Industries
East Fourth Street
Sovern, Pennsylvania 29405

Dear Mr. Beatty:

The opportunity to be associated with you and the Mako organization sounds ideal. It offers an opportunity to fully contribute to your challenging goals for future growth.

I'm familiar with your foresight and leadership in the industry, and your company's reputation for growth, professionalism, and dedication. My own background—and motivation—matches your stated needs for an exceptional, involved (function)* executive. (Give one or two examples of successful accomplishment.)*

Your interest would be most appreciated; I look forward to jointly exploring this unique and exciting opportunity with you.

                                        Sincerely,

                                        (Signature)
                                        (Typed Name)

Cover Letter—Answering Company Ad.
* Fill in your own function and accomplishments.

(Your Address)

(Date)

(Address)

Dear Ms. Berbery:

Congratulations on your recent appointment as Vice President of Nosedrop Industries, Inc. I am sure that you will enjoy the challenge of your assignment, particularly in view of the exciting expansion of your company earlier this year.

I'm familiar with your foresight . . . and your company's reputation . . . (see prior letter to Mr. Beatty).

Sincerely,

(Signature)
(Typed Name)

Letter to Newly Appointed Executive

(Letterhead)

(Date)

(Address)

Dear _____:

Thank you for your recent assistance and advice in my efforts to further broaden my career.

I'm happy to tell you that in early 1982 I was elected President of V.W.X. Company. This is a very high-risk/turnaround situation, but the experience promises to be challenging and very exciting, even if it turns out to be an interim assignment.

Since experienced turnaround experts and profit-improvers are hard to find, let's keep in touch!

Thanks again for your professional counsel and personal courtesy; it is most appreciated.

Cordially,

(Signature)
(Typed Name)

Thank You/Announcement Letter—Upon Taking A New Job.

Resume Printing Note

Resumes can be typeset, as in the case of the example that immediately follows. Typesetting can add a touch of class and style when properly executed.

The main drawbacks are the extra cost involved, and the fact that local printing businesses don't always have professional typesetting ability or capability.

Ask printers to show you various examples of their work, and select the style that produces the professional impact and impression you are seeking to project.

ANNE LIP

Home address: School address:

GOAL

To find a challenging, creative position in the communications field. Highly motivated. Newspaper, magazine, radio and television experience.

EDUCATION AND HONORS

Yale University, Class of 1983 (3.8 GPA), History major.

Scripps-Howard Foundation: Journalism Scholarship recipient (1979-80, 1980-81, 1981-82).

Poynter Fund: Journalism Scholarship recipient (1981-82).

Nationally published: _Saturday Review_ and _View_ magazines.

Hold Third Class Radio Operator's License with Broadcast Endorsement.

National Merit Scholarship Finalist.

PROFESSIONAL EXPERIENCE

5/81 - 9/81

REPORTER, _The Home News_.
Wrote extensively researched feature stories; covered local politics; and was responsible for the early morning police beat at this Central New Jersey daily.

5/80 - 8/80

INTERN, _Saturday Review_ magazine.
Copy editing, short book reviews, and article research; wrote SR Calendar and SR Recommends columns.

6/80 - 8/80

REPORTER, EDITORIAL ASSISTANT, _View Magazine_.
Participated in birth of major cable TV trade magazine. Worked directly with both editor and publisher on every aspect of the magazine; wrote major feature articles.

6/80 - 8/80

FLOATER, WPIX-TV and WPIX-FM radio stations.
Clerical work for New York television and radio stations.

COLLEGE JOURNALISM

10/81 to —   SENIOR EDITOR, _Yale Daily News_.

4/81 - 6/81   EDITOR, _Yale Daily News Freshman Issue_.

1/81 - 5/81   EDITOR, CO-FOUNDER, _The Liberal Dialogue_.

9/79 - 9/80   NEWSCASTER, Yale Radio Station (WYBC-FM).

1/77 - 9/79   NEWS EDITOR, Rutgers University Radio Station, (WRSU-FM).

OTHER ACTIVITIES

Yale Symphony Orchestra (viola); Yale Political Union; Viola teacher; Intramural sports: co-ed touch football, basketball.

Resume of Anne Lip

Chronological Resume

CHARLES DEMMING

(Address)
(Phone Number)

OBJECTIVE   V.P. Operations ... V.P. Manufacturing ...
Director of Manufacturing

SUMMARY   Profit-oriented professional manager
Given increasing manufacturing and problem-
solving responsibilities as career progressed.
Possess ability to motivate personnel and to coor-
dinate diverse functional areas.
Multiplant experience in both union and non-
union environments.

EDUCATION   MBA, Business Management, Tulane University,
1975
BS, Chemistry, Tulane University, 1967

EXPERIENCE
1976–   D.E.F. CORPORATION—GENERAL PLANT
present   MANAGER
Full responsibility for the corporate facilities,
multiplant (three shifts) and distribution operations of the large consumer products subsidiary of
a major corporation.
Due to reduced material losses, cost reduction
programs and work rule changes, productivity
has improved by 22% in addition to a favorable
budget variance of $875,000. Productivity gains in
packaging operations approximate 25%. Overall
budget responsibility totals $12 million.

Areas of responsibility encompass P&L, manufacturing, distribution, plant engineering, OSHA/EPA, maintenance, safety, purchasing, QC, capital improvements, and personnel (250 employees).

Product/process experience: Filling, packaging, and compounding for a line of 180 consumer products.

1970–1976   G.H.I. INDUSTRIES—GENERAL MANAGER

Involvement from plant startup to three-shift operation with 200 employees. Initiated personnel and equipment efficiency programs resulting in direct savings in excess of $500,000 annually.

Responsibilities included P&L, manufacturing, capital expenditures, union negotiation, purchasing, R&D, QC, OSHA/EPA, new product development, and customer relations.

Product experience: wallpaper, textiles, and coatings.

1965–1970   J.K.L. COMPANY—PLANT SUPERINTENDENT

Directed the efforts of 50 manufacturing and laboratory employees. Set up production standards and schedules, QC systems, and personnel training methods.

Areas of responsibility included manufacturing, union negotiation, purchasing, R&D, QC, and OSHA/EPA.

Products: industrial chemicals.

1964–1965   M.N.O. CORPORATION—LEAD CHEMIST

Set up and carried out laboratory and pilot plant experiments on heavy industrial chemicals.

Chronological Resume

SAMUEL S. PADE

OBJECTIVE   President ... Executive Vice President of a me-
             dium-sized company or division.

BUSINESS EXPERIENCE

October   <u>EXECUTIVE   VICE-PRESIDENT—EXPLE-</u>
1967   <u>TIVE PRODUCTS CORP.</u>
to   Hired as General Manager of Operations in 1967.
Present   Elected to Vice President in September 1968.
             RESPONSIBILITIES: Operating Officer with
             policy, planning, and direct line responsibilities.
             ACHIEVEMENTS: Implemented successful pro-
             grams in:
             Sales:
                 Organized company-owned Sales operation in
                 the Midwest. Hired manager, set and met ob-
                 jectives: sales rose 10%, profits increased 28% in
                 one year.
             Marketing and Advertising:
                 Established New Products program. New item
                 lead times cut by 50%; Lab and marketing
                 priorities programed on a routine basis. Rede-
                 signed two product lines.
             Customer Service:
                 Reorganized the national Service department.
                 Improved order handling; achieved make *vs*
                 buy savings of 60%; gross profits increased by
                 realistic pricing.
             Costs:
                 Established a formal profit improvement pro-
                 gram: over 300 projects worth $1,600,000 in
                 savings implemented to date.

Planning:
Organized an integrated system of production planning in a multiplant operation. Inventories reduced by $3,000,000, substantial improvement made in customer service.

March 1964   MANAGER OF INDUSTRIAL SERVICES—
to   LIBEL CHEMICAL COMPANY
October   RESPONSIBILITIES: Growth and Facilities
1967   Planning, Distribution; directed various management functions.
ACHIEVEMENTS:
Established central development lab and purchasing departments.
Achieved savings of $500,000 per year through centralized purchase contracts.

March 1961   MANAGER OF MANAGEMENT PLAN-
to   NING AND CONTROL—STAR CHEMICAL
March 1964   COMPANY
RESPONSIBILITIES: Design and installation of management control programs: Costs, industrial engineering, inventory control, project engineering, quality control, pricing, and product mix.
ACHIEVEMENTS:
Reduced workforce in major division by 25% using ratio delay study technique. Division subsequently attained standard *vs* previous experience of $50,000 loss per month.

June 1953   NEW PRODUCTS MANAGER/MANAGER
to   OF LONG-RANGE MARKETING
March 1962   PLANNING—SODAH POPP CORPORA-
TION

RESPONSIBILITIES: Managed the flow of new products from the laboratory stage through manufacturing; devised five-year investment and marketing strategies for all major product lines; directed wage incentive and cost reduction programs.

ACHIEVEMENTS:

Installed marketing planning function, working closely with product managers on product life cycles, marketing plans, competitive moves, and research developments. Successfully coordinated the introduction of 29 new products and improvements through research, marketing, purchasing, and manufacturing.

EDUCATION BA Boston University—1953. Major in Business Administration. Member of Varsity Fencing Team. Earned 100% of college expenses.

BACK- Graduate of Management Science Course (IBM);
GROUND Instructor at AMA Seminars; member of American Management Association, Employers Legislative Council of New Ohio.

Chronological Resume. This is a good example of a chronological resume with very specific accomplishments spelled out. Whether you are in sales or systems or any other functional area, this Accomplishments List is the way to get attention drawn to your specific and special capabilities.

Georgia Hamilton
500 George Avenue
New Haven, New York 12345
(300) 555-1346

SUMMARY
An experienced executive in distribution and manufacturing management, who has successfully operated in corporate and divisional capacities with responsibilities in manufacturing, distribution and personnel/labor relations, is looking for additional challenge and career growth.

JOB
HISTORY

1970–Present   P.Q.R., INC., Rahway, California
<u>Plant Manager</u>
Have total authority for plant management, including manufacturing, labor relations and personnel, production, delivery, and related support functions. Responsibilities include the training, motivating, and development of personnel, as well as the direction of all plant activity. Plant size is approximately 400 people. Accomplishments include:

Installed a plastic bottle manufacturing operation, instead of a buy-outside situation, which resulted in an annual savings of $100,000 per year.

Devised and initiated a safety program for tem which had previously been nonexistent. the plant. Also installed a plant security sys-

Annual cost reductions are in the range of $100,000.

During the first year, production capacity and volume was increased by about 9%, which resulted in a favorable plant variation in excess of $200,000.

Insured conformance to federal standards and agency requirements such as OSHA, DOT, EPA, FDA, EEO, and other related regulations.

Increased customer service to an all-time high of 98% plus.

Manager—Specialty Manufacturing

Accountable for two specialty manufacturing plants and three distribution centers. Major responsibilities were to monitor performance: service, quality, and productivity/cost unit. Further duties involved acting as chief negotiator at all negotiating sessions for a total of six plants, acting as an advisor to all plant managers in regard to labor relations.

Accomplishments:

Installed numerically controlled metal-working equipment realizing an approximate savings of $100,000.

In labor relations, assisted in a union decertification.

Manager—Distribution

Responsibilities involved the number and location of warehouses, inventory planning and control, customer shipment methods, and the car-truck fleet:

Introduced a computerized inventory control program. This helped to reduce the number of warehouses and required product inventory to a manageable level.

Initiated an in-house car and truck fleet management program that saved the company almost $70,000 per year.

1960–1970   S.T.U., Weldon, Massachusetts
Manager—Distribution Facilities
Responsibilities included branch packaging (15 locations) of consumer products and the responsibility for company-owned warehouses, as well as a large network of public warehouses. Achieved the following:

Reduced the number of warehouses and stock locations in the United States from 100 to 25. Inventories and related functions were reduced, realizing a savings of more than $350,000 per year.

Employment Supervisor
Responsible for recruiting technical and nontechnical personnel. Was associated with the Hay Evaluation Committee for the company.

EDUCATION State University, BA

Functional/Chronological Resume of College Senior.

RHONDA S. LAUGH

SCHOOL ADDRESS: HOME ADDRESS:
Rutgers B.P.O. 20425   15 Lane Drive
Post Office Box 1119   Easwest, New Jersey 08816
Piscataway, New Jersey 08854   (201) 257-5555
(201) 932-0181

CAREER OBJECTIVE	Immediate aim is to apply my versatile, hands-on industrial engineering/manufacturing experience. My long-term objective is to become part of the management team of a manufacturing organization.
EDUCATION	BS, Industrial Engineering, May 1980 Rutgers College of Engineering, New Brunswick, N.J. Cumulative Average: (A−)
HONORS AND AWARDS	Merit Scholarship from the Material Handling Institute Merit Award from the Society of Manufacturing Engineers Alcoa Scholarship for Summer Professionals Tau Beta Pi: National Engineering Honor Society Alpha Pi Mu: Industrial Engineering Honor Society Dean's list: all semesters

WORK
EXPERIENCE

5/79–8/79 <u>Plant Industrial Engineer</u>
Aluminum Company of America
Massena, New York
Performed comprehensive packaging projects, inventory analysis, plant methods and layout studies, rent *vs* purchase analysis, time studies, and related management projects. I worked independently, with little supervision.

6/78–8/78 and 6/77–8/77 <u>Engineering Department Aide</u>
Johnson & Johnson
New Brunswick, New Jersey
Handled manufacturing specifications duties.

ACTIVITIES

College of Engineering: I.E. Seminar Leader
Rutgers I.E. Department: Open House Coordinator
Tour Leader: for the Dean of the College of Engineering
American Institute of Industrial Engineers
Society of Women Engineers: Secretary

Functional/Chronological Resume of a Woman Reentering the Employment Scene. The 4/75 to 9/80 period was a part-time, family owned business. Since then she has had two temporary jobs. Yet this strong functional resume got her a good job as business office manager with a consulting firm.

(Name, Address, Phone Number)

SUMMARY

Experienced Accountant/Bookkeeper: numbers oriented, with a record of proven accomplishments.

Eight years of diversified industrial experience, with both large and small companies.

Particularly adept at maintaining and analyzing detailed data for accounts receivable, accounts payable, inventory accounting, and similar functions.

BA, Kings College, Economics Major, Accounting Minor.

SKILLS AND ACCOMPLISHMENTS

Control of intercompany order processing for a major branch of a Fortune 500 company, as well as stock control/coding/converting of returned goods data for IBM input.

Responsible for complete accounts receivable function, including preparation of statements.

Maintenance of complete order entry, purchasing, and accounts payable system.

Establishment of chart of accounts for small company; preparation of financial and tax statements.

Development of simplified bookkeeping systems.

Capable of successfully analyzing customer profitability by account and class of trade.

Experienced in preparation of fixed asset and depreciation reports.

EMPLOYMENT HISTORY

9/80 to Present	Temporary Accounting Assignments: Brunswick Company, Lambert Company.
4/75 to 9/80	Financial Manager: Portable Service.
9/61 to 4/75	Volunteer work: Treasurer, Budget Chairman, Auditor.
8/53 to 1/56	Junior Accountant: Chico Manufacturing Company.

Functional-Chronological Resume. Note that this is actually the resume of the same housewife who returned to work after many years, gotten some recent experience, and has now left out the first 20 years of volunteer and business experience.

(Name, Address, and Phone Number)

SUMMARY

Experienced Accounting Manager: numbers oriented, with a solid record of accomplishments.
Nine years of diversified business experience including financial management and cost control for a multicorporate organization.
Particularly adept at meeting critical deadlines, supervising others, generating and analyzing data for control reports and financial statements.

SKILLS AND ACCOMPLISHMENTS

Responsible for preparation and analysis of financial reports—balance sheets, profit and loss statements, and operating budgets.

Experienced manager of various accounting functions, including accounts receivable, billing, collections, and payroll.

Installed and managed a computerized accounts payable system featuring invoice control, aging, cash disbursement, and check printing programs.

Established new cost-accounting system featuring accurate job-cost identification of labor and materials.

Broad business background also includes tax preparation, cash flow, purchasing, sales analysis, and customer profitability studies.

EMPLOYMENT HISTORY

12/80 to Present	Accounting Manager: engineering company.
2/80 to 12/80	Assistant Business Office Manager: InfoMed
4/75 to 2/80	Manager (part time): Portable X-Ray Service

BA, Queens College, Economics and Accounting

Functional Resume.

JOHN BULLFRIGHT   10 Hoes Lane, Omaha, N.M. 09999
(555) 123-4567

<u>Objective</u>:   Responsible general management position with a consumer goods manufacturing company.

<u>Professional Background</u>

<u>Experienced general management executive</u> with a record of over 20 years of career growth and accomplishment in the areas of *profit-center responsibility/production/distribution/sales and marketing.*

Have progressed to General Manager and Vice President with responsibility for the operating management of a major division.

Personal attributes include the ability to build a strong loyalty from subordinates . . . a facility for rapid analysis of problems and opportunities . . . and the hands-on managerial skill for meeting stringent cost and profit objectives.

<u>Areas of Major Accomplishment</u>

GENERAL
MANAGEMENT

Reversed failing division into a profitable operation by installing profit-oriented controls over sales, lab, and manufacturing groups.

PRODUCTION

Widely experienced in improving plant productivity. Previous positions include Foreman—Production Supervisor—Manufacturing Manager—and Vice President.
Accomplishments:
Productivity increased by 35% in first 12 months.
Costs reduced by over $4 million, including $1 million in overtime.

ASSET
MANAGEMENT

Decreased inventory investment by over $3 million with a simultaneous 35% reduction in backorders.

PURCHASING

Centralized the purchasing function of eight semiautonomous units, yielding savings of $500,000 per year.

SALES/
MARKETING

Reversed the falling sales and profits of a sales operation by installing new account incentives and controls.

PROFITABILITY

Achieved four-fold improvements in sales by high-priority new product program. In another case, profits turned around by updating a mature product line.

Optional Page Two of Functional Resume—Giving Specific Dates and Names of Companies.

JOHN BULLFRIGHT   page two

Record of Career Growth

Vice-President of Operations
Fortune 500 Consumer Products Company
11/79 to Present
Productivity increased by 35% in first 12 months.
Costs reduced by over $4 million, including $1 million in overtime.
Inventory investment decreased by over $3 million.

Division General Manager
Tinkertot Company
12/75 to 11/79
Turned around failing division. Sales and profits increased 20% per year.
Improved plant productivity by 25% through improved supervision and scheduling.

General Manager of Operations
Joanfelt Products Corporation
10/67 to 12/75   Company officer for six years.
Coordinated successful new product program: sales volume increased fourfold during this period.
Installed new-account incentives: sales and profits climbed 28%.

Manager of Industrial Services
Papasan Chemical Company
3/62 to 10/67   Managed engineering, process development, profit improvement, and purchasing departments.
Centralized purchasing function: achieved savings of $500,000 per year through negotiation of blanket contracts.
Turned around division profits by updating a mature product line.

<u>Plant Management</u>
Wilkee Company
6/58 to 3/62   Also supervised the production engineering
and new product groups.

   Increased direct labor productivity by 30% in two plants.
Coordinated the successful introduction of 28 new products.

<u>Education</u>   Queens University, BA Degree; advanced
courses at Jonestown Graduate School of Business; graduate of IBM Management Science
Course.

Resume in Letter Format—To Companies or Search Firms.

(Letterhead)

(Date)

XYZ Company
(Address)

Dear _____:

I am a general management executive, highly motivated and results oriented, with a demonstrated record of success. Here are some examples:

Revitalized an outmoded network of plants and warehouses. Achieved almost $1 million per year in savings due to the consolidation program which eliminated two plants and five warehouses.

Designed and directed an inventory control system that cut total inventory investment by 38% in nine months.

Doubled plant output, and continue to direct attainment of new performance records for material usage, quality, and customer service.

Direct an aggressive cost reduction program. Over 300 cost savings projects worth $1,600,000 have been implemented, including improved machine efficiency, bulk handling, and distribution savings.

Consistently come in below budget and local averages in my capacity as chief company spokesman in union contract negotiations.

Participate in the development, corporate planning, and national launch of new products which have increased sales volume over 400% in a five-year period.

As part of the management team reporting to the President and Chief Executive Officer, share responsibility for corporate policy and actively participate in goal-setting and budgeting. Represent our company at Association meetings, in high-level negotiations with customers and suppliers, and in community activities.

I am currently employed by a medium-sized manufacturer of consumer packaged goods which is a subsidiary of a Fortune 500 manufacturer. Recruited in October 1970 as General Manager of Operations, I was later promoted to my present position as Vice President of Operations.

My previous experience was:

1960–1970   Midget Chemical Company, Manager of Industrial Services. $900,000 saved in two cost-reduction projects.

1955–1960   Dum Dum Chemical Company, Manager of Manufacturing Control.
Reduced manning by 25% and helped turn around the chemical division.

1950–1955   Ape Corporation, New Product Manager. Managed key projects in marketing involving the introduction of 24 new products.

I have a BA Degree in Business Management from Stamford University and have completed advanced courses at the Wharton School of Business.

I am writing to you because of my interest in relocating with another firm. The reason is our parent company has recently cut back our development and growth funds; they plan to divert all available money and attention to their own sales efforts.

Thus, on a confidential basis, I intend to seek a challenging association with a company which can benefit from my results-oriented management experience. I hope to consider a number of alternatives during the next few months at an appropriate salary level of about $50,000.

I am free to relocate and to travel. My primary criteria are a chance to demonstrate my worth and, upon effective performance, the opportunity to move into general management.

A personal interview would permit further discussion. I am confident that I can produce the same profitable results that I have attained for my present employer.

Sincerely yours,

(Signature)
(Typed Name)

E L E V E N

WRITING TO COMPANIES

Your most successful tactics and attention-catching materials will not spring full-grown out of your brain. Rather, they will be developed and honed by trial and (mostly) error, through constant testing in the marketplace.

For most job seekers, your best bet is to follow the steps previously outlined: get your written materials together and, as an early rehearsal/trial, start limited (100, not 1,000 or more) broadcast mailings to companies, headhunters, and in answer to ads.

This chapter will guide you in your initial corporate mailing campaign. As a reminder, this mailing approach:

1. Is often both the first and last word from the so-called experts.
2. Is not an end in itself, although it could actually dredge up some hot leads.
3. Is primarily a chance to refine and rehearse your letters, resumes, and interviewing techniques.

If you follow this approach, however, you will have a dual opportunity.

1. A long-shot at a job, through a small broadcast mailing and testing campaign that should improve as you go along.
2. An opportunity to be completely professional, polished, and ready when you go on to hit your prime corporate targets directly (and more personally).

The objective, then, is to test your materials and thereby to turn the odds more in your favor.

Turning the Odds

The company tactics table previously given estimated that reading incoming resumes may help fill anywhere from 0 to 25% of the corporate openings. With a little imagination and personalized attention, you can write to certain of these companies (along with the 100 other job seekers who will also write) and get that 25% working for you and that 0% working for everyone else!

The first step in turning the odds in your favor is to carry out some research in order to find a personalized hook. The key to such personalization is to keep your eyes and ears open—read journals, personnel announcements in the newspapers, listen and follow up on industry rumors, and so on.

Here are a few examples of personalized hooks designed to catch attention.

You Need Me (*Find an opening, pinpoint the problem, and offer your services.*)

"I noted the recent change in your reported profits, and I know I could make a specific and immediate contribution to that money-losing subsidiary you just inherited . . ."

Mutual Acquaintance

"Joe Fink is a mutual acquaintance, and he suggested today that I drop you a line . . ."

Play on Vanity, Similar Interests

"I read your recent article . . ."

Zero In on New Program

"I'm a standard cost expert, and I understand that you have a standards program about to start . . ."

Hit Someone New (*they'll often bring in their "own" new crew*)

"Congratulations on your recently announced promotion to Vice President of Research. . . . I have . . ."

Specialized Interests or Products

"Your company's current interest in radio-controlled hockey pucks leads me to . . ."

Find your own hooks for as many companies as you can. For those companies with no apparent hooks, send them a good broadcast-type letter addressed to a specific executive.

Test Mailing

Here are the basic steps in planning your mailing campaign to companies.

1. Decide on the number of companies to be test-mailed initially. I suggest 50 to 100 as a maximum. Then go to the library and make up your mailing list: name of executive, title, name of company, and address.
2. Pick the most suitable information-gathering approach: by industry (Advertising Red Book); geographically (state industrial directories); by company

name (Standard and Poor's or Million Dollar Directory); by trade association (membership directories); by executives' names (directories of officers and directors or various *Who's Who* volumes).

3. Decide if you want a short letter plus resume, or a two-page tailored-to-the-target letter with no resume. Both will work; select the one you can do the best writing job on. The paper size can be full page or on smaller Monarch size paper. (Monarch is better for short cover letters.)

4. Write at least five different drafts of your letter.

5. Let your spouse, a friend, or an interested executive proofread all five versions, to help clean up one of them. Put the letter aside and don't think about it for 24 to 72 hours.

6. Repeat step 5 two more times, at a minimum.

7. During the open review time available in steps 5 and 6, write your resume. You always need a resume. Even a two-page, detailed letter will, at best, be followed up by a request to see you and/or your resume. (Remember, write your own resume: it not only helps you see how good you are, but the sophisticated reader will spot a "professional" job immediately, and you lose points for that.)

8. Mail them all out at once.

9. Check off all answers on your address list.

10. Respond very promptly to all requests for a resume, salary information, or other data.

11. In three weeks, send a different follow-up mailing to all people on the list who have not responded. If the overall response to the first mailing was good, you can refer to your first mailing. If it was poor, change the paper color, typeface, and so on, and don't refer to the initial mailing.

12. Then, write to 50 or 100 more companies, with any improvements you can or should make, based on what you learned from the first set of companies.

Further Notes And Suggestions

1. A 2% positive response is average. Positive response means a specific request for more information, a resume, or an interview.

2. All letters should be original typed copies. Try to avoid offset letters with a "matching" typed-in address: the "matching" will usually be noticeable, and is a negative factor. Print shops with word processing machines can handle this job properly for you—the machine rapidly types the standard portions of the letter, and the operator enters the variable data (address, etc.) as required. You will find that the reader likes to think that you admire him, respect him, and know he is an individual, not just a title. Thus the urgency of neatly typed personalized letters addressed to a specific executive.

3. If there are a few target companies that you have your heart set on, resist the temptation to include them in this initial test.

    (a) In all likelihood, your first resume mailing will be the very worst in your entire campaign. (Later on, you'll look back at your first letters and resumes and laugh.)

    (b) Instead, such prime targets deserve your most personalized research, attention, and efforts. As covered elsewhere, your best bet is to develop a friend inside the company, or a friend with a contact inside the company, and to call—not write.

    (c) The next-best approach outlined here is to do

your initial broadcast testing and research, and then later write a targeted letter to the prime company, rather than sending them your standard, still-untested, initial mailing piece.

4. Testing Reminder: This is a test-mailing campaign, so that you can learn to do even better as you go along. As you refine and improve your materials, test them again with 100 different mailings, and again, if necessary, to the same (or different) companies.

5. Always use a pure white or light beige paper stock, of good quality.

6. The first page of the letter can have a printed personal letterhead if a top-level job is involved, but do not use your present company's business letterhead.

7. The envelope must be marked "Personal and Confidential" or "Private and Confidential."

8. Don't put your name and return address on the envelope. This is a turnoff before the envelope is even opened. Such personal or nonbusiness envelopes almost *always* signal a resume is enclosed. If you have a list with old names or addresses, and want to see what is not deliverable, you should put your return address, but not your name, on the envelope.

9. Your letter must be short, literate, and attention-grabbing.

    (a) Try to avoid a first sentence such as: "Enclosed is my resume of my business experience . . ." That is over-used and unimaginative.

    (b) Instead, the first sentence or two must be a 1-2 punch: a hook for grabbing their interest, a few words on who you are and what you can offer. See the specific examples in Chapter 10.

    (c) Be low key: do not brag, oversell, or otherwise blatantly proclaim how wonderful you are. Your reader knows that these are just biased words you wrote on a piece of paper about yourself. It sounds both desperate and conceited, a terrible combination.

(d)   Instead, talk about the target company, your background, and what you could bring to the blessed union of you and the company.

(e)   Never beg for a job. Don't even hint at being anxious for a job. Instead, be low key, mature, polished.

Generally, if the company can offer you some legitimate career advantage, do point it out: a growth industry, a more varied product line, a bigger challenge, an opportunity for professional growth, a match with your education or experience, and so on.

(f)   Don't list any references, either in your letter or in your resume. Only give them when you are asked specifically. And make sure the references know in advance that their name has been given, and to whom.

(g)   Don't provide any information on your salary or expected salary. It can do you no good. It could hurt if it's too high or too low.

10.   Your resume must be one or two pages, well written, professionally printed, with your objective stated at the top.

11.   The worst times to mail are in June, July, and around major holidays, particularly the month of December. The entire job market is quiet during these periods.

12.   Make sure you have your telephone covered during the daytime: Companies may only call once or twice during business hours, and if there is no answer, you could lose some important leads.

TEST MAILING TO SEARCH FIRMS

B efore discussing the details of this phase of your test mailing, let's examine these particular recipients of so much time, money, and attention. Executive recruiters, sometimes called executive search consultants or headhunters, work exclusively for corporate clients. The recruiters' fees are entirely paid by these clients. The recruiters' assignments are to fill certain key job openings in their clients' organizations.

There are two types of recruiting firms. The most prestigious is the guaranteed fee type, which sets a fee that the corporate client must pay whether an acceptable candidate is ever hired or not. The contingency type operates more as a high-class, fee-paid employment agency: the company pays the fee only if an acceptable candidate, recommended by the recruiter, is hired.

A Leading Source of Addresses.   Recruiting firms can range from good to sloppy, since in many states no licensing is required. Membership in various professional associations is one clue, and this data is given in the leading source of headhunter addresses, *The Directory of Executive Recruiters,* published annually by Consultants News, Templeton Road, Fitzwilliam, New Hampshire 03447, (603) 585-2200.

Search Firm Test Mailing.   To get a head start on planning your test mailing, go back and reread the Test Mailing to Companies section in Chapter 11, and adapt those steps as follows.

1. Select 50 (or a maximum of 100) recruiters on your list for your first test mailing.
2. Check the previously referenced book appendices for breakdowns by industry, specialties, and geographic location.
3. to 10.   Same as the company checklist: Choose resume *vs* resume-letter format; do five drafts; redo each at

151

least once or twice; mail out all together; check off answers; respond to requests.

11.   In four to five weeks, send a new/reworked follow-up mailing to the list, except for those who already have contacted you for an interview. Do not consider it a contact if you get an acknowledgment form letter in response; it must be a request for an interview.

12.   Retest by mailing to additional 50 or 100 headhunters. Send a newly revised version, if first mailing had few positive answers.

Notes and Suggestions

1.   A 2 to 4% positive response on both the first and second mailing is average. Positive response means a request for more information, a copy of your resume, or an interview.

2.   All letters should be original typed copies. For higher-level jobs, avoid offset letters with a matching typed-in address. Headhunters look for that, and are not impressed when they see it. Word processing can help you keep the costs down. Also, never use paste-on address labels; the address must be typed directly on the envelope.

3.   There may be some recruiters who seem to be ideal targets, due to their reputation, specialty, or geography. Save these prime targets until you know your materials are right. That is, wait to see how well your first test mailing goes. If you get a 7% or greater positive response, you have a better than average package, and can hit these prime targets immediately thereafter.

4.   Use white or light beige paper of good rag-content quality.

5. Printed letterheads on your cover letters are optional: they may be called for in a top-level job situation.

6. There is no need to mark envelope "Confidential," as was suggested for direct mailings to companies.

7. Feel free to include your name and return address on the envelope. Note that this is opposite to what you should do when writing to a company executive. Headhunters expect to receive letters from individuals. Moreover, some do tend to move, merge, or go out of business, and your postal returns will show you which addresses to cross off your list.

8. For the job market in general, and these mailings in particular, the worst months remain June and July, and around major holidays.

9. Set the proper tone. Headhunters are a rare egotistic breed; they like to think they can supply their clients with the finest candidates in the country, those who may not even be on the job market and, preferably, are not. So your letter has to be low key, not desperate. The tone should be (don't use these words, of course): "I'm not really desperate, but I might consider responding favorably to a new challenge or more money . . ."

   (a) Thus, your cover letter should be short and an attention grabber, but don't oversell, brag, or beg. Give no references. (See the samples in Chapter 10.)

   (b) Do feel free to tell headhunters your salary and extra compensation such as bonus, profit sharing, options, or company car. This is opposite to the advice given on writing to companies: Companies can be scared off by money, but headhunters can't begin to operate *without* it.

   Don't lie about your salary. But do interpret as

favorably as possible any type of past payments and the like that can be considered bonuses.

10. The headhunter's primary tool is your resume. He prefers not to even think about you unless you have one, or can work one up quickly. This is admittedly inconsistent and contrary to their stance that they deal with people who are *not* in the job market, but—that's how it is in the real world.

So, even if you initially mail out a grabber of a two-page letter, also have a formal resume ready. If there is any interest, the headhunter is sure to call and ask for a copy of it immediately.

11. Headhunters, if they do have any interest or questions, prefer to pick up the phone and call. If there is no answer at the number you have provided, there is less than a 50-50 chance they will write or try to call you at night.

So, make doubly sure that the telephone number you provide in your mailing has some sort of daytime coverage. Either have a responsible family member available or else arrange for an answering service (the same ones that doctors use). If such coverage is just not possible or economically feasible, buy a telephone answering machine. These machines "turn off" some callers, but that is still better than potentially missing most of the calls.

ANSWERING ADS

155

D on't think your job search will be solved by answering the help-wanted ads. Statistically, few jobs ever appear in ads compared to the total openings in the market, and also: a very low percent of job seekers ever get their jobs by answering ads.

Read and answer ads by all means, but don't tie up all your time—or hopes—on this exercise. Once you decide to try it, be sure to answer any and all ads that you could even remotely qualify for. Do not be put off if they ask for a certain educational or experience background. Few, if any, candidates will fill all their requirements anyway—it's always a compromise.

If there is a specific fit, and you have the time, tailor your cover letter to each ad's requirements. But, don't invest all your time in this, since ads are nowhere near as productive as some of the other techniques described in this book.

When to Mail

Mail later, not earlier. It probably makes sense not to mail your response the day the ad appears. Most people do, and yours could get lost in the flood. Actually, no one buys the first pair of shoes they try on or the first resume they see, so nothing is lost by coming in a few days later. Furthermore, on an important job, no one rushes to fill the job the first week or so anyhow, so there is little chance of missing out.

Salary Information and Ad Follow-ups. Don't give any salary information, even when it is asked for. Let them decide first if you are of interest. A too-high or too-low salary can only turn people off, so why risk it?

For every ad that you get no response on, be sure to send a follow-up letter (or letter and resume) in two to three weeks. Make it a new and different letter (and resume too, if you have one available).

Five Tips on Finding Ads.   There are five major places to look for Position Available Ads:

1. Display ads in *The Wall Street Journal* for your region. These are primarily found in the Tuesday (and Wednesday) editions.

2. Display ads in large metropolitan newspapers, primarily in the Sunday editions.

3. Smaller display ads in trade magazines and professional society journals, which usually are published monthly.

4. Display and classified ads accumulated from all four *Wall Street Journal* regional editions, published weekly by the *Journal* as the *National Business Employment Weekly*. It contains a week's worth of Position Available ads for executive, managerial, and professional positions at salary levels from $25,000 to $250,000. (Available at larger newsstands or through the mail; see ads in the *Journal.*)

5. Classified ads in each of the above sources. These will normally cover jobs up to about $25,000.

Ads and the Confidential Search

If you are trying to keep your job search a secret from your current employer, be very careful about answering blind ads that give no clue as to who the company is.

It is not uncommon for word to somehow get back to your boss. It could mean instant dismissal, so be very careful; if in doubt, don't do it.

EMPLOYMENT AGENCIES

Many employment agencies normally work on volume and turnover. They're concerned with the quantity of jobs and referrals, and not necessarily the quality of their matching service.

On low-level jobs they may try to collect the fee from you. But they can be used free of charge, and in some cases can give you help if used correctly.

Tips on Using Agencies

1. Write or call a few if you are in the low to middle salary category, say $10,000 to $40,000 range. Insist on company-paid opportunities only; these are called fee-paid positions. This eliminates the expense that you otherwise would be responsible for.

2. Try to find agencies that specialize in your career field: education, quality control, engineering, sales. Look for their ads in technical journals, specialty magazines, and so on.

3. Seek out those that adequately cover your geographic area or your particular industry.

4. Visit a few that have a reputation for being professional and able, as opposed to being paper-mills. Personal contact with an interested, heads-up job counselor can give you:

    (a) Insight into the market (and how well the agency covers it).

    (b) Tips on how to sell yourself.

    (c) Perhaps, first choice of any first-class openings that may cross his or her desk.

5. Don't waste too much time filling out reams of their forms—just say "refer to resume."

6. Don't get carried away by pressure tactics, particularly:
    (a) Promises of lots of jobs: that's sometime used to keep you from going to other agencies.
    (b) Pressure to accept any job, or to drop your salary requirement. They often want to place you quickly and collect the fee, and not necessarily make a wonderful career match.

Agencies perform a useful service in the disorganized, haphazard world of job openings and job seekers. Just keep in mind:

Agencies don't usually handle upper-level jobs.
You must learn how to use them—don't let it become vice-versa.

Agencies and the Confidential Search

Be careful: If your paper (i.e., your resume) is being circulated by a flock of agencies, word could get back to your company. Most companies consider that an act of treason, punishable by firing.

FIFTEEN

YOUR STRATEGY FOR TARGET COMPANIES

You don't need 125 job offers. You don't even need 15, especially if none of the 15 are what you want. You really only need one, two, or three suitable offers from the right companies.

Thus, after you've had sufficient, successful practice with test letters, resumes, and hopefully some interviews, you should cut out the Mail-A-Bunch broadcasting approach. You're ready to move to an individual campaign aimed at your 1, 2, or 20 top target companies.

By now, you've completed your list of target companies that you think may be for you, so it's time to tackle your first two targeting problems:

1. How to learn more about each target company, including its inner workings and need for your specific talents.
2. How to make contact with the key decision maker inside the company, to let him or her know of your potential contributions.

Both of these problems can be solved in one shot by your first-level contacts. Free of charge and with far less hassle than with an agency, your contacts can help you learn about the target companies' products, organization, personality, and needs, plus they can provide you with key employee names. If you don't yet have an inside contact, hopefully the names your first-level contacts provide you with are those of inside decision makers.

If not, don't worry—this obstacle, too, is overcome easily. Simply try for the names of any lower-level people in the company who might steer you to the decision makers. Another gambit is to ask all your contacts for the names of still others (competitors, salespeople, leaders in the industry) whom you might call to get the names of key target-company hirers.

At any stage of the contact chain, there's no need to beat around the bush or resort to devious tactics to ferret out this indispensable information. Simply be straightforward and tactful: "A pleasure to talk to you . . . Would you know what companies need help in (my field)? To whom can I talk within (the target company) that might have an interest in solving the problems of . . . ?"

Thus, aside from names, ask first-level and subsequent contacts to supply you with one additional piece of information: problems that the key contact or target company are wrestling with. See what their needs are, and position yourself as the answer to solving those problems.

You can probably think of examples of operating problems on your own. As you well know, all companies have problems. There may be departmental frictions, or people that are poor performers. The company may be falling behind in an important area of the market or technology or, conversely they may be struggling to keep up with an unprecedented growth situation. There may be a political battle going on or just ended in their executive suite. So, gather your intelligence data: there have got to be problems you can help them to handle!

Other Research

Don't depend solely on your personal contacts to keep abreast of what's new in your target companies. Do some homework so you can talk intelligently to your contacts, and ask them leading, informed questions. This includes:

1. Studying the company in your local library's business and stock market reference department.
2. Reading the "New Appointments" section of business papers and trade magazines. These are regular features in most sectors of the business press.
3. Tuning-in the rumor mill in the industry. Suppliers' representatives are great sources for this type of information.

Once you determine your target company's problems and get the name (if not an introduction to) the key decision maker, it's time to get into action.

Telephoning the Decision-Maker or Key Hirer

The executive that we call a key decision-maker or key hirer is someone who is up high enough in the target organization so that he or she:

Knows of the organization's problems

Has some responsibility for solving those problems

And has the power to make an employment decision even though there may *not* even be an official "opening" as such.

That is the person you need to reach! You can do this the easy way or the hard way.

The **easy way** is to get a personal introduction from a mutual friend (this could be someone that a first- or second-level contact has referred you to).

Here's a sample script: You just call and say, "I was talking with Joe Doaks recently; he's fine and sends his regards. Joe asked me to give you a call when I had a chance. He thought it might be worthwhile if we had a chat about my background— perhaps over lunch next week or a drink at Charlie's Bar after work—to see if there was anything in my experience that might help you with the XY problem. I've always had an interest in your company, and I would like very much to learn more about your operations. So when Joe suggested . . ."

The **hard way** is a "cold call": You telephone that unknown key hirer.

All you may have is his or her name and title, plus the name of whoever gave you the name in the first place. The intermediate referral person may not have even known you (perhaps he was a referral on the phone by one of your first-level contacts). He may not even know the key hirer either, at least not on a personal basis. In that case, remember that the colder the call, the colder your reception will be!

But cheer up, all is not lost. The answer is to warm up your approach as much as possible. This means that, to the fullest extent that you can, become a known quantity! Name-drop as many people as possible that are known in the industry. See the following section for some examples; it covers "writing," but the same principles apply.

Writing

If you can't call for some reason, then write a letter to the key hirer. Attract his attention in the first sentence or two by addressing an issue of personal or business interest to him. Name-dropping is vital; examples include:

"In a discussion last weekend with Jim Smith of the ABC Company, he suggested that I contact you . . ."

"In your recent talk before the Bolt Association you mentioned the industry-wide problem of metrification. James Hutt, President of the Association, suggested we might get together and exchange some ideas on this . . ."

"I'll be leaving (or have left) the Famous Alpha Company, and Jim Baccus, a knowledgeable man in our industry, suggested that we should chat. He mentioned that you have an interest in entering the nut market, an area where I have six years of low-cost manufacturing experience." (This can even work if you have no personal reference, but your old company is well known or thought of. Call a competitor and tell 'em who you work for.)

Telephoning vs. Letter Writing

A telephone call is more effective than a letter—always! Once a target hears your voice, you immediately/almost magically become a better-known quantity. If you are well-rehearsed and confident enough, it will be tough for him to turn you down.

Compare that with a letter: The best response you can usually hope for is a thank-you form letter, perhaps with a standard request for a copy of your resume for the file. Unless, of course, your letter refers to a sure-fire, mutual friend he respects so much that he has to see you, at least out of courtesy.

But if you have, in fact, such a powerful mutual friend, don't waste time with a letter. Call or, better yet, see if you can't get that friend to personally call the key hirer on your behalf!

Breaking Through the Telephone Barrier

Yes, a telephone call can pave the way to that new job you want. But there are problems. Specifically, how do you:

1. Talk to the key hirer?
2. Or, get past his overprotective secretary?

In answer to 1: Don't be shy, and don't act as if it's a cold call, even if it is. Be natural, be confident, pretend your original contact-reference was 100% sincere in saying that "you *should* call . . ." For specific openers, try any of the ones already suggested for either letters or telephone calls.

The answer to 2: A secretary's job is to screen the boss's incoming calls, and protect him from the likes of you, insurance salespeople, and other time-wasters. But you also have a job to do: to get through to the boss. Some suggestions are given here. Stop at each one; only go on to the next if you still hit an impasse.

1. "Art James, a mutual friend, suggested I call Mr. Bossly."
2. "It's a personal matter."
3. "It's such a top-level matter, only Mr. Bossly, not the Personnel Department, is directly involved or interested."

If the above doesn't work, don't lose heart. There are other ways to reach your target.

4. Send a short letter, as described previously, and add "I will call you next Thursday." Then call him. If the secretary tries to block you, just say "Mr. Bossly is expecting my call."
5. Try calling between 8:00 and 9:00 A.M., or after 5:15 P.M. Few secretaries are on duty at those times, but many bosses are.
6. If all else fails, send a telegram, Mailgram, special delivery or registered letter—ask him to call you, or ask if you can call on a certain day. Then use the line given in 4 on the secretary.

Cost-Effectiveness Note

Save the phone calls and telegrams for your 5 or 15 prime targets. Otherwise, you can easily run up a very large bill for these services if you were to call 50 or 100 companies nationwide.

Key to Success

This chapter is one of the shortest but most important in the entire book. All your groundwork up to this point was designed to make this step as easy and natural as possible. So pick up that phone—you use it every day—it's your direct line to success.

Do it, today. You won't get interviews by sitting in your chair and reading! You must reach out.

No one can physically hit you through the telephone wire.

The telephone is an everyday miracle: you can actually talk to someone miles away that you might never otherwise meet.

Since he or she can't hit you, don't pass up the use of this underrated miracle of personal communications. Reach out and touch someone—for a job!

SIXTEEN

MASTERING THE INTERVIEW

H ere's an important point in maintaining overall perspective: the first 15 chapters were not an end in themselves, but merely a preamble to this one. Because, in the end, there are only two key campaigns in the war to find a job:

1. Getting an interview. That's where all your contacts, resume, and writing campaigns were aimed: just to get you a shot at a job interview.
2. Winning the interview itself. It won't be the most qualified candidate who gets the job, it's the one who can convince the hirers that he is the most qualified.

Ultimately, everything is directed at the interview, because no one is ever hired for a job without meeting face-to-face with the prospective employer.

When you do get an interview, it's a good sign: it means you have your foot partly in the door. And, that they have a potential opening (not necessarily for you).

But with the claustrophobic, paranoid, and depressed state you are in from desperately searching for any type of an opening, the offer of an interview can cause a rush of adrenalin, a rash of manic dreams, high-soaring exultation, and boundless optimism.

Hold it right there: if you go overboard emotionally, you will be sure to ruin the interview. You may march in smiling but unprepared, absolutely convinced by their interest in you that they will instantly and permanently desire you, your mind, and your body. Or else, just prior to the interview, you may suddenly remember that you have been rejected by hundreds of companies (at least through the mail), and that you don't really know what to say, how to act, where to begin, or why they would ever want to hire a disorganized mess like yourself.

But there is a happy way out: you *can* prepare for everything, including an interview. By and large, an interview is as ritualistic as a Mass, as predictable as any business meeting, and can be more fun than a game of Twenty Questions. But only if you are prepared for it, that is, know the ritual, the general agenda, and the questions to be asked.

To get the full benefit of this chapter, you probably should read it three times. First, skim it quickly to acquaint yourself with the interview's ritual aspects. Then, skim it a second time to understand more fully and to appreciate the many tips on how to handle yourself. Third, with the help of a spouse or friend, concentrate on giving completely rehearsed answers to some tough questions, delivered with a friendly smile and relaxed bearing.

The Known-Quantity Interview

Before getting into the rules that apply to all job interviewing situations, be mindful that being known is one of the most important rituals you can put to work on your behalf:

> Both you and the interviewer will be more relaxed if you are already known to the interviewer. Even if it's only through "a friend of a friend."
>
> Your reception will be less formal and the questions asked will be less penetrating when you are there under such favorable circumstances.

If for reasons of time or mixed-up communications the interviewer is not fully aware of your inside or outside connections, be sure to mention them as soon as you possibly can.

Name-Dropping Examples

"I'm grateful to good old Dick Clark for setting this up."
"Bob Stanton sends his personal regards."

"Bob Jones gave my name to your boss; they are old golfing pals, and my name came up last Saturday at the Club . . ."

"I'm very familiar with your company: Jim Krow of United International has been calling on you folks for years and Stan Pat of ABC, Inc., a mutual friend, knows your Jim Burk and his people from the Bikechain Association meetings. . . ."

The moral is clear: name-drop as much as you can!

There may be other interviews where you have no personal contact to refer to. Try for any point of mutual interest:

"Your company is very highly regarded in this area/this industry."

"I read that *Business Week* article on your president, Mr. Branton, . . . he must be quite a dynamic leader. . . ."

Whether you have a contact or not, there are universal rules of interviewing that you must keep in mind. These are covered in the next section.

25 Tips: How to Act in an Interview

1. Be prepared: know the company. Study the company's background at your local library. Ask people you know about the organization, people, products. The interviewer will be very impressed if you casually mention some item of note that you saw in their annual report or in Standard & Poor's.

2. The first few moments are the most important. You *must* smile, look him (or her) in the eyes directly, give a firm handshake, and act confident.

3. Be on time.

4. Don't be nervous. The interviewer often is; put him at ease.

5. Dress properly (more on this later in the chapter).

6. Observe the offices, trophies, pictures, and so on; look for clues; something to ask about or compliment.

7. Don't oversell: let him want to buy you. Don't ever forget: He's been told to look for good people, he wants good people, he's hoping you will be good people!

8. Be a listener. Don't overwhelm the interviewer; don't talk too loud. Try to find out what and who he wants: "How can I help your company—what's the problem?"

9. Be brisk, clear, and concise. Don't ramble. Be sure to rehearse all tough questions. And don't slow down the interview by asking him to read copies of your best memos or reports: if the materials are exactly pertinent to the job, you may offer to leave your exhibits with him at the end of the interview.

10. Stay cool: don't interrupt or argue. If you don't understand a question, ask him to repeat it, please. Take your time in answering an unexpected question. Think it through.

11. Be friendly, sociable, and conversational. (But of course don't tell a young interviewer "when I was your age . . .")

12. Be poised and at ease under pressure. (But *no* joke-telling.)

13. Know your field and your job. Volunteer to expand on any answer, but don't be dogmatic or inflexible.

14. Be prepared to show your experience and drive. But you are not there to recite your job history—you are there to win his confidence.

15. Look for an opening, then give a "canned" (memorized and rehearsed) short talk on your success story.

16. Be diplomatic, yet ambitious.

17. Tell the truth, but don't volunteer bad news.

18. Be enthusiastic, energetic. (The older you are, the greater the need to radiate stamina, energy, vigor, and action-oriented drive.)

19. No smoking, gum chewing, nervous tapping, or darkened eyeglasses.

20. Be yourself—be honest, sincere. They are looking for someone who is trustworthy. Evasive answers are an immediate turn-off.

21. Don't be so relaxed that it comes across as nonchalance or lack of interest.

22. Don't knock anyone, particularly at a previous company. Try to be positive.

23. Put off all salary discussion until the very end. Don't get specific, there's plenty of time later to negotiate.

24. Never accept a job offer on the spot; ask to think it over.

25. Remember the odds: you will usually need five or more interviews in order to get one job offer. Don't allow all your hopes to ride on one company or one interview.

Need for Rehearsal/Preparation

There are no shortcuts to public speaking, or knot tying, or sailing: it takes practice! So will this. To prepare for an interview you must write, memorize, and rehearse the following:

1. Answers to tough questions. Ten samples are given in this chapter. (Also see Appendix IV.)

2. A one-minute talk on what you have done that could successfully be applied to the job under discussion. Borrow this from your resume and also toss in some examples that didn't fit on your resume.

3. A minimum of three questions to ask the interviewer. For example: questions on the division's size, products, the job or department, or the whereabouts of the previous incumbent on the job. This is further covered below in answer to question 9, "What do you want to ask me?"

Before we rehearse though, let's discuss how to dress for the interview.

How to Dress

For a non-showbiz interview, that is, a normal office or managerial job, a man's best bet is to wear a dark, conservatively cut suit that is well-tailored, clean, newly pressed, and fits well: not too tight or loose, with cuffs and sleeves just right. Also a conservative tie, not a bow tie, a white shirt (with no frayed collar or cuffs), clean nails, recently cut and well-groomed hair, high dark socks, a minimum of jewelry or rings, and well-polished shoes. No fancy belt, or buckles, either. Women should dress in a similar, conservative fashion: nothing sexy, all business. Avoid faddish styles, spike heels, jewelry, heavy perfume or makeup, loud colors. Stick to classic suits and skirts.

Two additional dress tips for everyone:

1. If you carry any packages, a coat, or umbrella into the offices, leave them outside with the receptionist or secretary.
2. Plan to arrive early if you have been traveling for a while. Ask the receptionist for directions to the restroom, and take a few moments to re-examine your hair, tie, and so on.

Also, spend some time outdoors—get some healthy color in your cheeks.

Ten Tough Interviewing Questions

As already noted, be prepared and rehearsed for your one-minute success talk, and for questions such as those that follow. Prepare for any other questions that you can think of. In that way, if any of them are asked, you are ready and can relax. (If they are not asked, you can also relax.)

Thus, by being confident and prepared, you can relax and enjoy the entire interview. It's a game, and should be enjoyed as such.

1. "Why are you leaving your present job?"   Avoid getting into personalities or conflicts, even if that is the real reason. (It usually is!) Instead, answer (without hesitation or eye-blinking) with a rehearsed, career-building: "I want to make more money." Or: "I'm looking for more professional challenge." Or: "My boss is young (or new), and the outlook for a promotion is five years away." Or: "My present job or department is very narrow in scope, and I've ceased to learn and grow."

There are other, slightly less satisfactory but perhaps more applicable answers, such as "A new management team has been brought in," "Our industry is in a decline and many layoffs are expected," or "Our entire department was transferred out, and ten people have been asked to leave or else be immediately transferred to Moscow, Idaho."

2. "What can you bring to us?"   Mention your drive, integrity, experience, and business sense. If more of an answer is needed, that's easy too. Assuming you did your homework, you will know if the company is growing, or is unprofitable, or lacks market research, or has a particular product or service that you have expertise in. Your rehearsed answer should speak to satisfying their need, with one or more specific examples from your successful experience.

3. "What company or boss or job did you like best? least? Why?   There are a number of questions here, so be prepared in advance with your answers. For the "like best" questions, you might answer, if applicable, "all my companies /bosses/jobs, because I had an opportunity to learn from each one, and to grow, contribute, and develop my craft at each step." For the "like least" questions, keep away from personalities; concentrate instead on "There was little challenge or no growth at the ABC Company, due to market conditions."

4. "What are your strong points? Also, tell me your areas that need further development (i.e., your weak points)?"   This is your opening, your opportunity to give your one-minute canned talk. To prepare: reread your new resume—it should tell you precisely who you are and what you can "bring to the party."

Give a quick example as you describe each of your strong points. For example, "I am a self-starter ... I planned, directed, and installed a new standard cost system. I am also an expert on government bid business. On one project I was able to ..."

As for your weak points, the safest are those such as "I drive myself very hard," that is, those that are normally considered assets. Others include: "I'm a believer in completed staff work, and insist that all projects be thorough and oriented towards the decision-making process." Or, "I'm sometimes very impatient, and like to get the job done correctly, but in the least possible time."

Don't volunteer any really bad news, at least not in the beginning interview. Once you have sold yourself to the company you can reveal, if you choose, your past fling in a nudist colony or your winning bout with alcohol. Of course, if there is a chance that the company already knows of your problem, you can elect to admit it up front very openly. But for the most part, your weak points are none of their business—after all who expects a truly honest answer to that one?

So, if you absolutely can't stand small details (every job has them, of course), you can always equivocate this weak point with "I'm best at program planning and installation, but I'll need some help to handle the detail work in analyzing your 60,000 different subassemblies."

5. "Do you think you have the right type of experience to handle this unique job? Aren't you over- or underqualified?" If you are a plant management type with no interest in sales, and the job under discussion turns out to be a sales job, say so! But if you feel you want or could handle the job, then explain how you have handled other challenges successfully, and have sold yourself and so many of your projects consistently.

In any case, if you are interested in a job, state that "I know I can do the job, and do it well—so I am neither over- nor underqualified."

6. "Please explain the time gaps on your resume. For example, you left Consolidated Universal on 1/15/79 and didn't join General Engine until 6/20/79. What happened in the interim? Be prepared in advance with an answer to all such time-gap questions. Perhaps you were considering a return to school, or starting your own business.

In fact, if you are out of work for an extended period, you might consider doing some limited part-time consulting for the money, the potential business connections, and the continuity of your job record.

7. "Where do you want to be in five years?" Show that you aim high. Look for a mimimum of 10% to 20% salary growth per year, and a much better title, perhaps the title of the boss you would report to.

8. "If I were to ask your wife (or neighbor, or former boss) about your strong points and weak areas, what do you think they would tell me?" This is a transparent attempt to get you to play back your self-image, by pretending to allow the words to come from someone else. Just give your canned positive and negative answers already covered in question 4.

Don't even try to guess what your wife or boss would really say—how would you know, or the interviewer either, for that matter?

9. "What do you now want to ask me?" As covered earlier, you absolutely must prepare at least three, and probably four or five, questions on the interviewer's:

(a)   company
(b)   products
(c)   problems
(d)   promotional opportunities
(e)   the interviewer's background
(f)   his impressions of the company
(g)   what happened to the previous incumbent of the job now under discussion?

10. "Do you think you might be interested in joining us? Why?" Don't answer: "Yes, you bet, because I'm out of work."

Instead: Give a positive reaction to the career opportunities the interviewer has described, assuming you really feel there is a possibility of a match. Give a specific reason why, as well: the boss, the work, the challenge, the company, and so on.

The good news about this question is: it usually comes near the end, and if the interviewer's body language, perceived interest in you, and voice tone are positive (begging, or hopeful) when asking this question, it usually indicates an above-average interest in maintaining you as an active candidate for further consideration. If, however, it is asked merely due to routine or out of politeness, don't get too excited. So, listen and watch for positive interest in your answer.

If there is a genuine eagerness to get your positive reaction, and you in turn are interested in the job, then give the following answer: "Yes I am interested in the job (or challenge, etc.), because of . . . Is there any chance that I *can* be considered an active candidate for the job?" The directness of this answer will almost always reveal the interviewer's exact frame of mind and your odds of being actively in the running!

And now, one last easy question you'll also mess up (without preparation, that is). This is a seemingly easy but extremely common type of question, and an interview-wrecker par excellence. It can take several forms: "Tell me about yourself." "Tell me about the various jobs you've held." "Tell me who you are—what kind of a person—your childhood, your schooling and your jobs."

Without proper rehearsal, you will undoubtedly mess this up completely:

1. You may start with your early childhood, and cover far too much unimportant detail. The interviewer, after all, has no real personal interest in your life story, so don't be flattered and tell all about your first day at school and your dog named Skippy. Don't be boring.

2. You can also destroy the timing and tempo of the interview by an overlong verbal autobiography. Fill the limited interviewing time with a few salient facts: There are always interview time limits and limited attention-spans, and the interview's give-and-take balance could be permanently destroyed by an overlong, monopolizing (and non-pertinent) discourse on your part.

If you are fresh out of school, or you sense that a few words on your childhood are definitely being called for, spin one or two short, soothing tales like: "I had a normal childhood, growing up in Kankakee, Illinois," or "I was born in California, and spent most of my growing years in New Jersey, where I went to high school and on to college." Then, go immediately to your most recent or applicable job experience.

It is possible to "tell about yourself" and yet sufficiently cover your first 20 years in one or two sentences. If the interviewer is a prying amateur psychologist, throw in the words "normal childhood" or "happy childhood." Otherwise try to get to your most impressive and/or a recent period as quickly as possible. If it was college, you can dwell on that—your favorite courses, and so on. If it is your current job, try to cover all your earlier jobs in a sentence: "My 20 years of work experience covers four companies, mostly in advertising on the client side, and I've recently had two or three exciting projects I'd like to tell you about, if there is time."

Note what we have done in the last two paragraphs: we have covered a total of 40 years in two sentences, and asked for permission to talk about what we really want to cover—some recent and impressive success stories.

The worst that can happen is for the interviewer to interrupt and ask "were your mother and father really understanding?" Be sure to smile and answer "Yes." Or, you might be asked to start your business story with your second or third company instead of the most recent. Since that is on your resume and hopefully is also engraved in your memory, start wherever requested, and remember to recall with fondness the "exciting challenge" and "job satisfaction" you derived from the two or three projects you proceed to tick off with aplomb.

Games Interviewers Play

1. "Seatmanship."   Amateur psychologists and people with large offices may play a game called "pick any chair you wish," or Seatmanship. The interviewer stands or sits behind the desk,

doesn't wave you to a seat, but instead waits for you to take either the chair squarely in front of the desk, or a second chair to the side of the desk. My advice is to summon up your nerve and take the side chair: it's literally less of a direct confrontation in every sense of the word. A side chair is less formal, and doesn't allow the full expanse of the desk to intimidate you, or keep you at too far a distance.

2. "Advanced Seatmanship."   There's one interviewer I know, a personnel consulting Ph.D., who will subject you to a course in "advanced seatmanship." This involves two chair choices: a very heavy, high-backed chair located a distant 20 feet in front of his desk, or a small, very low sofa 10 feet to the side of his desk. Let's consider your choices. The front chair is much too far away for comfortable discussion. The sofa is too small for 2 people, and is also far from the desk. If you select the sofa anyway, it turns out to have such deep cushions that you sink down and can hardly sit up straight, much less talk intelligently, since your knees are now pressed squarely against your mouth.

In cases such as this, there is no correct or "right answer": the point of the whole exercise is to observe your calmness, self-confidence, and executive decisiveness when you are first ushered into the office. My own suggestion is to greet him, shake his hand, ask for permission to move the front chair next to the desk, and then confidently move it. This is sometimes easier said than done, by the way. This particular interviewer apparently has an unusual sense of humor, and has built in a second obstacle to further test your poise and determination. That far-out front chair, which you so confidently thought of moving, weighs at least 50 pounds and is stolidly sunk in his 4″ deep shag carpet. As you wrestle mightily to move the overweight chair you are carefully watched, partly to observe your poise, and, I suppose, partly because it is a hilarious scene to him; much like watching someone slip on a banana peel that he deliberately left on a sidewalk. But remember, to him it's just a psychological test or game.

3. "Testmanship."   To handle the other, more routine, types of written or oral psychological tests, merely pretend to yourself that you are normal, ambitious, had a happy childhood, and then give them *that* answer. It's an insidious and privacy-invading game, their quasiprofessional peering into your brain, so play it as a game. Sure, do this seriously and carefully but, inside, maintain your sense of the humor during all this probing and dodging.

4. "Jacketmanship."   Here's another interviewing ploy. You are walking to the corner office of the big-boss/interviewer and you notice that no one in the offices you pass is wearing a jacket. Suit pants, white shirt and tie, yes. But all the shirt sleeves are turned up one cuff's worth, and the jackets are all hanging on chair backs. The boss is apparently an action guy, you see that from his hyperactivity, shirt sleeves, rapid speech, and his sports trophies, so he is obviously the one who sets the style standards.

And there you are, sitting up ramrod straight in your best suit and cleanest shirt, wondering if this shirt-sleeved dynamo will think you are too stiff or formal to fit in, or too stylish and effete to "roll up your sleeves."

The question is: should you take off your jacket? Here's some suggestions:

If the office is hot and humid, ask the interviewer if you can take off your jacket.

If you do decide to ask, whether it's hot or cold, early in the interview, ask permission confidently, and then effortlessly remove your jacket with as much nonchalance as you can muster.

If you have any doubts, such as, "Taking it off is over-obvious pandering," or "I'll feel my buttoned-up self image diminish if I do," then don't consider early removal of your jacket.

However, even in the latter case, you may later sense a growing trust and a relaxing of defenses as the actual interview unfolds. Your intuition can guide you at that point.

Summary: "If it doesn't feel right, don't do it." That is, if at any point you feel that taking off your jacket is too melodramatic or phoney, don't do it.

5. Other Psychological Games.   Here are four other stress-type games that the interviewer may try.

A. *Keep You Waiting.*   This may or may not be deliberate. Relax, don't freeze up or get mad. Ignore it. Smile.

B. *Phone Interruptions.*   It's bad manners on his part to accept calls. Ignore it; just make sure you remember what the topic was before the call, and go right back to it.

C. *Long Periods of Silence.*   It's often a trick. Don't think you have to fill every time gap. Do ask if there is anything else he wants to know. Play it cool, and don't panic or blurt out something for the sake of saying something. Relax and wait for the next question if you have nothing further to say.

D. *Asking "Anything Else?"*   Another trick. After asking you a tough question like, "Why did you leave your last company?" he may (seemingly) know that your answer was only part of the story, and ask you, "Anything else?" Only reveal what you want to reveal. If your answer "lack of challenge" isn't enough, have a (rehearsed) second part ready; for example "The company's sales were in a decline and they were in a holding position." Don't go any further if you don't want to, even if he again asks, "Anything else?"

6. Personality Ploys.   These are not games, just personalities doing their thing:

> *Friendly:* Rambles on forever.
> *Egomaniac:* Rambles on about himself.
> *Reserved:* Doesn't open up at all.

Suggestion on all three: get the interviewer back on the track. Without taking over the whole interview, attempt to build some sort of structured plan into the proceedings. For such a three-part structure, see the following section.

The Three-Part Interview

Interviews can be broken into three parts:

1. *Opening.* Sets the overall mood, tone, aura. Probably as important, if not more so, than any other part. The reason is that the interviewer's first impression of you will most likely be his lasting impression. Remember your opening gambit: You *must* smile, look directly in eyes, give a firm handshake, and appear interested and confident.

2. *Heart of Interview.* Primarily for exchange of information and firming of opinions. The potential employer will be trying to make three simultaneous evaluations:
   (a)   If your personality will fit in.
   (b)   If you could be an asset as an employee.
   (c)   If you will reflect well on the interviewer if you are hired.

You must give the interviewer a feeling of warmth and comfort that you can meet all three of these criteria. Also, plan to use this period to actively discover if the job and company are of real interest to you. Plus, you'll want to try to pry clues out of the interviewer to discover just who and what they want. This is very important! Don't be afraid to ask, "What are your problems?"

3. *Final Portion.* Try to accomplish these goals at the end:

   (a) Show your interest.

   (b) Express your thanks.

   (c) And, if not covered thus far, ask "Where do we have a fit? Where do we not?" or "What is the next step?" or "Am I in the running?" This type of clinching, final question shows your interest, and is similar to the earlier one: "Is there any chance that I actively can be considered a candidate?" This is a good way to elicit their interest and to size up the odds of your being considered further.

   (d) Look for the signs that the interview is over: shuffling papers and no more questions. Don't overstay or prolong it. It can't, won't, and shouldn't go on forever.

Interview Follow-up Tips

1. Each interview must be followed up by a personalized short letter within a day or two. The letter should thank the potential employer for his time and interest; should reflect your appreciation for the information gained; and contain a short "sell" message on your interests, your directly related background, and on a specific challenge they face that you could help them meet successfully.

2. If no word is heard within two weeks, telephone the interviewer and ask if "a decision has been made yet."

   The call will show your interest and enthusiasm. If you call, you may also determine from his tone of voice if you are still in the running.

3. Don't go into shock if you are turned down later, after a seemingly successful interview. Most interviewers try to hide their true reactions while you're sitting there. If you are told that you are not an active candidate, you should then ask what strengths you would need to develop in order to become a future candidate. That's an excellent way to find out what turned them off to you. It's not often that you have this feedback opportunity to find out why you have been rejected, and this is the best time to try.

4. If you sense per your follow-up call that there is some active interest in you, but no decision yet, then call again in a week or two.

5. After any of these calls you should also send them a letter—even if they have indicated that you are probably out of the running:

   (a) If you judge that they need a reminder of one of your strong points, or

   (b) If you can think of some new (or previously not mentioned) reason, or personal attribute, or experience that they should know about.

You can't just give up now—not when it's so tough to get an interview. Hit them again!

Some Final Tips

1. Read a book on body language. You'll discover that his finger tapping does mean he's bored, and his leaning away from you means he doesn't want to hire you.

2. Have someone, perhaps your spouse, read each of the tough questions to you. Try to answer them, after some rehearsal, without using any notes. It's not enough to initially write down the answers. You must be able to speak them smoothly, briskly, and without any eye blinks, pauses, tics, or flinches. With a smile, whenever appropriate!

3. Also have them review and rate you on the 25 How to Act tips listed earlier in this chapter.

4. Try to smile whenever you can!

5. Watch your first impression and don't be nervous. If *you* don't choke up, the interviewer can relax too, and you'll both feel better.

6. At best, you'll only win 1 in 5, so relax and loosen up. You now have the materials and the know-how at your fingertips for learning the art of interviewing. If you follow the winning advice in this chapter, you will be miles ahead of anyone else in your spot who tries to "bull" his way through.

7. If you are overweight by more than 10 pounds, either go on a diet, get a brilliant tailor, or else resign yourself to the fact that heavyweights usually don't get too many job offers—very few at the upper levels.

8. Otherwise, forget about your looks, age, sex, or whatever—they are only looking to hire someone good. So, give them a reason to want to hire you.

No One Can Keep You From Success—Except You!

*If you plan on defeat, you will achieve defeat. If you think you can't win, you won't. If you plan to succeed, you will. If you can build strong faith in yourself, you can stride up any hill. And that's what life's all about: if you pick your goal, and **think** you can, you'll make it—**without** any doubt.*

If you have self-doubts, if you have been fired, if you need a booster shot of enthusiasm for your clobbered ego, then read one or more self-help books: *Your Erroneous Zones* or *Psycho-Cybernetics* are good places to start. So is *How to Make Winning Your Lifestyle,* and *How to Be Your Own Best Friend.* These books, and others like them, can boost your ego, show you how easy it is to tune your thoughts to success patterns, convince you to make friends with yourself (you is all you've got, but it's a lot), and show you the no-guilt way to being a winner.

SEVENTEEN

STARTING THE NEGOTIATION PROCESS

J ob negotiations start at your very first contact. For example:

If you mail an initial letter boldly stating your desired salary, or perhaps admitting you are currently unemployed, the hirer immediately knows something about your possible salary flexibility.

Or, if you show up at any interview with a self-conscious hangdog look, you are directly telling the interviewer that you aren't sure if you *can* deliver on any reasonable job, or at any salary level.

The point here is simple: If you leave all your negotiating until the very last interview, you may give away, too early in the game, whatever cards you may be holding. That leaves very little room for (a) negotiating for a decision on their part to make you a firm offer, or (b) for dickering at the end for the salary and fringes you really want.

Successful Negotiations

The best description of a successful negotiation is where the parties walk away after the deal is struck, each believing he got what was important to him. Consider this example.

Tom has hungry chickens, and you have some feed to sell. If you are both reasonable, some sort of deal can always be negotiated. Tom could either sell his chickens, or swap some of them for feed, or else buy some feed for cash. You could buy or swap his chickens, but prefer to sell him the feed for cash. Depending on how strongly each of you feels about chicken selling or swapping *vs* a cash sale of feed, and the price of any of these options, you can eventually strike a deal that meets both of your needs.

This is not a Zero-Sum game as in a coin toss (heads I win) where the winner takes all. Zero Sum is from the Theory of

Games, and means that for every coin that I win, you lose the same. Thus, +1 and −1 = O, or Zero Sum. Successful negotiation is the art of having both parties feel that they won. That's the type of negotiation that must characterize all your job negotiations.

Let's Not Talk Money Yet

There will be some preliminary advice about negotiating in this chapter, before we actually get around to talking about salary, bonuses, fringe benefits, and so on. Be assured, however, that's where we'll end up.

Let's talk about where money fits into the various stages of job negotiating.

Initially there's a fact-finding period, and next comes the selling jobs: you selling them that you are the leading candidate, and them selling you that the job is attractive. Once the company wants you for a job and you want the job, the selling negotiations are two-thirds done.

At some point the selling blends into a third stage: negotiating. They now want you, but at a reasonable cost and as soon as possible. You want an unreasonable price, at a time convenient to you.

Thus, the three key phases are: fact-finding, selling, and (dollar) negotiating. Your object is to keep these three phases in their proper order, and not give the company any reason to get turned off early in the game while each side is still fact-finding or selling.

Moral:
Don't discuss specific salary until they are actually sold on you. Only then will you have some strong cards to play. It is then, and only then, that you negotiate for the specific compensation and working conditions you want.

Negotiating Strategy for Winners

There are three limiting factors at work in winning any type of negotiations: time limits, knowledge limits, and the power factor.

Normally, each side wants to bring the negotiations to a successful conclusion as quickly as possible, based on full knowledge of their own (and their opponent's) strong cards, and to win it on their own terms.

Let these factors work for you, not against you. You are not begging for the job; it's got to be a two-way street. You are entitled to make your best deal, so go for it.

Time: Don't be pushed into making an instant decision, particularly on an initial offer; always ask for a few days to think it over carefully.

Knowledge: Do your advance homework, then look and listen carefully. Knowledge in this case is power, since you'll know something about their priorities and needs.

Power: If they know you are out of work, they may try to exert the tantalizing power of a potential job—any job—at any salary they pick. Similarly, if you ask for too much money, they may try to counter with the power of precedent: "The job is already rated at a salary level 15." Don't let them push you around with that—precedents were made to be broken.

Everything is negotiable. You have power too: "I'm the ideal candidate . . . look at my background, experience, and results . . ." However, negotiating is always give and take. Just because everything is negotiable doesn't mean that you'll get everything—or anything. In the end, the terms will be a compromise, but in the highest sense of the word: both sides will be willing to live with the terms. It's a joint, happy agreement or balanced consensus, and not blackmail, a sellout, or an indentured servant contract.

Reminder: First Things First

All our Interview Tips, resume and letter-writing advice, and so on, are slanted towards helping you put your best foot forward. You must come across as a desirable candidate from the start, so that you can sell yourself continually and, ultimately, negotiate on offer frame-of-mind on the part of the company.

The Modern Selling of Yourself

People who are unfamiliar with the corporate purchasing function have a misconception of modern purchasing negotiations: they think of it in terms of a Middle Eastern bazaar atmosphere where the price is argued, threats are exchanged, and wild claims made. In fact, the selection of a supplier is based on more or less equal parts of quality/price/service. These factors are weighted by a competitive evaluation of past performance plus any commitments made for future quality, price, and service.

The final selection of a job candidate usually is carried out with the same balanced approach. Thus, you want to come across as a dependable candidate of good quality, who can provide the needed service, at a price within competitive limits. If they are sold on you, you will have solid Negotiable Strength.

Once they wish to buy what you have to offer, you will find that there are many areas in which to negotiate. Taking the purchasing example, the job candidate should know what every good purchasing agent knows: *Money And Everything Else Is Negotiable!*

A professional purchasing agent always negotiates more than just the price. He also attempts to negotiate payment terms (i.e., when the item must be paid for); cash discounts (for prompt payment); quick service response (perhaps having the supplier keep the item in stock in a nearby warehouse); mode of transportation; who pays for the transportation and/or insurance; who pays for the handling costs if defective material is received and/or used; quantity price discounts; guarantees of price protection for some period of time; return privileges if item is not used up or needed after all; warranties and guarantees; order cancellation terms; trade-in privileges if a new model comes out; and many other terms.

It's probably a much longer list than you thought, because most people assume that all these terms are standard. But something is only standard if you allow it to remain unchallenged.

Moral: Negotiate for anything and everything you want: salary, paid insurance coverage of all types from dental to disability, company car, job title, size of office, number of secretaries, size of staff, special pension benefits, areas of direct line responsibility, employment contract or temination agreement, club membership, stock options, bonuses, vacation schedule, expense account, and so on.

Timing of Your Demands

Timing is everything in life. When it comes to compensation negotiating, good timing is particularly important.

1. If you start dickering too soon, before they are ready to buy, you can blow the whole deal.

2. If you wait until very late, and show no interest in establishing your wants, the employer may assume you'll be content to take whatever may be offered to you.

3. If you hope to wait until you're on the job to put the finishing touches on your needs, forget it! You lose 99½ to 100% of your bargaining power the moment you accept the job. If you haven't negotiated that fancy company car or some extra vacation before acceptance of

the job, don't expect anything more once you show up for work.

Signals That the Time Is Almost Ripe

How to tell if the potential employer is getting serious:

1. You are called back for additional interviews, with additional people to meet, more time spent with them, sometimes followed by an offer of a plant tour.

2. You are asked questions like "Do you think you would be interested in joining us?" or "How much notice would you have to give your current employer?"

3. Other clues include: "Can we send you to a psychologist for testing?" or, "Can we have a list of references?" Say "yes" to both. If they happen to believe in testing, nothing will convince them otherwise.

   As for references, only give names after you have talked to the references, warned them of what is coming, and prepped them on the major strengths you think they should mention.

4. Note if the potential employer's tone of voice and body language has now become open and all sell. The previous prying and testing is replaced by an unmistakeable look of admiration. They seem to be saying to themselves, "He's good—let's try to sell him on the company and the job."

5. If an executive recruiter has been involved, after about the second or third interview he may ask you to meet with his client. This can be an excellent sign: you are undoubtedly in that select final group of two to four candidates to be recommended.

   The semi-bad news is that the recruiter usually has a favorite or leading candidate among the two to four finalists, and you may be one of the persons brought along to make his favorite look good by comparison. However, the client may still like you better, so definitely cheer up.

Also, the recruiter usually will let you know, after you have met the client and he approves of you, that you are an active candidate. If he doesn't, be sure to call the recruiter and ask about your status.

Note: If you haven't been "very interested but playing somewhat hard to get" until now, this is certainly the time, albeit late, to start. That is, play it cool, interested, but never overanxious or desperate.

Don't Stop Your Search Yet

At this point, keep up your job search; the game isn't over until you are actually on the payroll. Slip-ups do occur.

Perhaps the hiring executive can't get all the necessary OKs.

At the last minute the president insisted that an insider (his brother-in-law) get the job.

One of your business references is a neighbor of your boss-to-be, and has spread the rumor about you and that petty cash mix-up, or that pretty secretary.

The economy slumps again, and the company suddenly slaps a freeze on all hiring.

The rumors in the industry say you have just about hired on with someone else. When the rumors hit this company, they figure you are rigging a bidding war, and they drop any further thoughts of hiring you.

Moral:
1. *Don't stop looking.*
2. *Keep your contacts a secret—Gossip always travels fast.*

EIGHTEEN

CLOSING THE DEAL

T hey want you, and now it's a matter of you accepting/wanting them. After some discussion, let's assume that the title, responsibilities, and other points are understood and agreed upon jointly. However, money matters are still up in the air.

You do have some money cards to play: "I'm the best for the job . . . I'm a hot property and unique . . . Forget salary ranges, that's for average performances."

So, let's review in more detail how the money game is played, and some of the rules.

The Company's Initial Salary Offer

The company starts with your last or current salary, and/or the market value of the job:

1. First they compare you with their own official salary grade/level.
2. They also compare you with the previous incumbent's salary.
3. They may add something if the job is an obvious step up for you, or if you are way below the market.
4. They will subtract something if you are currently out of work, or too far over items 1 or 2.

And that's how they set their salary offer: their best guess.

The Company May Adjust Its Initial Salary Offer

After the first few resumes or interviews, the company may discover that to get anyone good requires that the salary range offer be raised, often by a substantial amount, if they are really intent on getting a top-notch candidate.

Then You Come Along—Asking for More

By the time you finally show up, the company has pretty much made up its mind:

1. That latest range should be satisfactory and fair to any and all candidates (this means you).
2. They are tired of explaining to the bosses "upstairs" why even more money is needed.
3. Yet, you do manage to raise some cogent points on the money issue.

Setting the Record Straight, or: It's Cogent Points Time!

As soon as you first sense any type of serious salary discussion coming up, you have to make sure the company understands your point of view:

1. "I'm the best for the job. I'm unique, and bring added dimensions, strengths, and contributions not visualized when you set up the job, or when it was handled by the predecessor."
2. "I'm a wanted, hot property." (No, don't actually say that—but be sure to infer that you might possibly have a number of other, active offers.)
3. "Anyone making a move like this needs a 20- to 30-percent increase to make it worthwhile. And that's on the average" (Everyone knows *that!*")
4. "If I sign on, I'm sure you would want me to feel that I made the right move, and to be positive and happy about it. I can't do that if your offer is at a rough parity with my current or last salary (that is, within 10 percent or so . . .)"

5. "So, please make it easy for me to accept, with an offer that is fair and attractive. I'd like to work for you, if possible."

Remember, then, to set the right tone just before an offer. This is your big ploy, graciously spoken just prior to the verbalization of their offer: "I hope that your offer will be such that you will make it easy for me to accept."

Once the Money Offer Is Made

1. You can always say "no thanks" if the offer is insultingly low.
2. You can always say "you have not made it easy for me to accept" if the salary offer is below the borderline of acceptability.
3. You can always say "well, perhaps the fringes and some sort of guaranteed bonus may make it seem more attractive," if the salary offer is almost OK.
4. You can even say, if the salary offer is terrific: "It sounds pretty good, but let's discuss some of the fringes in detail."

   But you must never say: "It's terrific . . . I love it . . . I accept right now . . . It's a deal . . . It's more than I expected . . . It's more than I'm worth . . . Can I start tomorrow? . . ."

You are never allowed to do that; it goes against the Law of Leaving a Loophole. You owe it to yourself, your family, and the company to consider any offer very carefully.

1. Ask for a few days to think it over and to discuss it thoroughly with your family. This shows you are a careful (as well as considerate) decision-maker.
2. Once the specific offer is made to you, there is little risk that it will be withdrawn inside of two days. After all,

the real decision to be made is: Should you accept their offer?

3. Best of all, asking for time is a skilled negotiating gambit on your part. Let them sweat while you take time to consider other offers, or to think of something else to sweeten the pot. Or, perhaps something you too-quickly overlooked (a loophole) during the exciting announcement of their offer.

Thus, you have nothing to lose and everything to gain by asking for a week (or at least a weekend) to discuss it, to sleep on it, and perhaps to think of more things to ask for or to clear up.

Nonsalary/Fringe Negotiations

Immediately following the first salary offer, make sure they (at the least) list all the fringes, and give you explanatory booklets on each fringe. That way you can go home, study the coverage, and be prepared to ask for any addition, or for the amounts of coverage you would like to have.

The Importance of Fringe Benefits

The fringe-benefit cost in some large companies today totals up to 50 percent of the base salary. To set that in its after-tax perspective: If your regular salary is taxed at 50%, and the fringes are not taxed, fully one half of your total after-tax compensation is in the form of fringes. (Example: $1,000 per week salary and $500 weekly fringes before taxes. After taxes, this leaves $500 salary and $500 fringe, a 50-50 split.) With that kind of financial impact, you can't afford to just sit back and take the minimum or standard benefits that are offered to everyone.

Of course, negotiating for salary is easy, compared to opening up the complex subject of personalized fringes. Salary is clear, clean-cut individualized, and usually has a specified upper limit. A dollar is a dollar, and so the amount of salary you are asking for is at least clearly understood and measurable.

Not so with fringes. But do not fret—it is often easier to negotiate in grey areas. It will pay you to find out all you can in advance from such items as proxy statements, as to stock options, deferred payments plans, incentive payments, and pension plans.

Your Fringe Benefit Shopping List

The amateur shoots for a high salary—period. The cool professional knows, before negotiations even start, what his potential asking list is, within limits of course. If there is sufficient salary, it will cover a multitude of fringe short-falls.

You being a cool professional, it's time to compile your shopping list, assign your priorities, and to identify your "must" items:

1. If there are stringent rules against dental insurance, for example, because of precedent-setting obsessions, you can only press the issue so far, no matter how many kids with braces you have.

2. However, older executives with no prior/vested pension rights may not be productive and happy on a new job with only a 10-year minimum vesting provision, and should strongly consider asking for some sort of special retirement consideration, inside or outside of the regular plan.

    No such consideration is ever given after you start, so get it on your "must" list if it applies.

The same applies if you *must* have three weeks vacation to start, or a severance-pay guarantee if the move is risky, or if you need moving expense money or tax help. Put it on your initial list.

Timing

If you have any such further demands, you should ask for them just as soon as the salary offer is made or, at the very latest, after the few days you requested to think the offer over. If you don't ask by then, you won't get anything additional at all.

Should You Accept Their Offer?

Obviously, the answer depends on the entire circumstances of both your search and their offer. You must consider whether or not:

1. You are jumping into a roaring fire from a merely uncomfortably warm frying pan.
2. You can get a better offer elsewhere.
3. You have any other leads left.
4. You got your minimum goal of X-percent increase, and/or your minimum fringe benefit needs.
5. You would be happier in a different job or in a different city.

Try to get three offers, so you can compare them. Consider the long- and short-term aspects: salary, location, advancement, boss, competitive climate, sales and profit trends, industry, risk, pressures, and so on. Pick the one you'll be happiest with.

Prying An Offer Out of a Company

If an interesting company seems ready to make you an offer, but is dragging its feet due to bureaucratic inertia or other problems, try to get them to hurry—particularly if you want to get two or three offers simultaneously in order to compare them.

Here's what you say: "I have an immediate obligation to answer this attractive competitive offer, but I'd much prefer to also have you make an offer—because *that* would certainly help me make up my mind really quickly!"

The Wrap-Up: Acceptance of an Offer

Once an offer is made and the final terms are agreed to mutually, make sure to ask for a copy of the offer in writing. This is normally in the form of a letter to you, stating your title, responsibilities, salary, starting date, and fringe benefits. The purpose is to prevent any misunderstandings:

at a later date when the company representative may be long gone;

and immediately, too: there is no use quitting your present job if that glowing offer is reneged upon unexpectedly by the boss of the executive who made the offer;

and also to make sure you know all the conditions as well. After all, you may not want to "give notice" quite yet if you must first pass a tough physical or get an A+ from all your references.

Once You Accept

You must now be all smiles, a member of the team, with no reservations or bitterness over conditions not won. Once you accept, you must be 100% sold, or at least appear to be.

Counteroffers

Don't even consider for a moment the idea of forcing a counteroffer out of your current company, or of accepting one if it's offered. It never works out, not for more than a month or three, so forget it.

Giving Notice and Other Good Things

Give your current employers, if any, as much notice as is reasonable. They may elect to toss you out the same day you give notice. Try to be aware of that possibility beforehand, and make flexible arrangements with your new employer so you can start sooner if you want.

Don't try to fulfill your dreams of marching in and telling your old boss where to shove the job. You may need that boss as a reference some day, plus you don't want him bad-mouthing you in the industry.

Clean out your desk and take only your personal things. That does not include project analyses or other materials that you wrote for the job; that's company property.

Promise to stay in touch with old friends, and do so. Alumni-luncheon meetings are not that rare today. Since business contacts are always important in getting ahead or in getting a job, stay in contact with prior bosses and executives. You may need their help (or vice versa) some day.

Say Thank You

Don't forget to write a short thank-you note to all the contacts, friends, and executive recruiters who made any effort to help you in your search. Let them know where and when you start, and that you appreciate their involvement, help, and counsel. Keep those contacts open at all times!

Vacation Time

I told you not to take a vacation when you first started out on your job search program. Well, with an airtight offer in hand, now is the time to do it. Get a good rest before starting out on your new job—you'll need it, and you deserve it!

SHOULD YOU CHANGE JOBS?

Or: What Do You *Really* Want To Do?

T his is an unusually disquieting chapter: it tells you some of the reasons you perhaps should *not* change your job at this time (assuming you have a choice.) Or, if you have already been fired, it explains that you may not be in the best shape to make a sound decision, not without some help, counsel, or deep self-analysis.

Just when you thought you had a sure-fire program that could win you a dream job, we drop this on you. Sorry, but it's for your own good.

Case Study I: Your New Dream Job

Let's say you just got a new job, and you started yesterday or today. For the most part most new jobs are more fun and more money. But not all the time. Here's some sad news about your new job that isn't working out:

You've probably discovered you made a big mistake after only two (up to a maximum of 16) hours on the new job. This is very typical, but very sad nonetheless.

That's right: You couldn't tell after 18 hours of interviews, but now, after only two hours in your new office, you see what an idiot you were to accept this job!

There are a few morals here someplace. Next time, try to get advance information from current or ex-employees or the prior incumbent. Ask to talk with various people at all levels, not just with the vice president, before accepting.

Maybe you should call up your old boss *quickly,* and ask if you can come back immediately! (Not a bad idea.)

Or maybe, just maybe you didn't know why you wanted to change jobs in the first place, or where you wanted to go, or what you wanted to do.

Case Study II: What *Is* Your Real Reason for Wanting to Change?

Now we'll take a case where you haven't left your old job as yet. Let's say you've been on the job with your old company for some time, and suddenly you get a new young boss. You're blocked for promotion for at least two years, maybe longer. And now you feel that you have to leave immediately. That's OK to tell an interviewer, but it should not be 100% convincing to you.

This is often a cop-out, a rationalization, a comforting story that you'd like to believe, but you know deep down is not the underlying real reason.

Real reasons usually involve such grubby topics as: personality conflicts; a political war with you on the losing side; insatiable desires for instant money and power; boredom with the job or company; a mid-life yearning for a whole new career; lack of ability to work for any boss/father figure; lack of constant appreciation from management for both you and the job you have been doing. Opportunity for advancement can thus cover a multitude of less shiny reasons, some of them reflecting your own inner feelings or abilities.

Before you change jobs, then, remember that a new job won't necessarily change the inner you. As cases I and II both illustrate, you'll drag all your problems and hang-ups with you to your new office.

Your Options

Upon reflection, you may discover that the underlying reason you want to leave is that you haven't played the political game very well, and you have been passed over for promotion as a direct result.

One realistic option then becomes: stay awhile and learn to play politics with the grownups. Make the boss look good, boost him behind his back, keep him informed, and at least appear to do better work to those who count. It might work!

Another underlying reason may be that you discover you are merely unchallenged and bored, and your attitude is showing—to your detriment.

There are some options here, too, if you are not on the firing hit-list yet. Let's assume for the moment they have already fired you, and someone new has just taken over your job—filled with unbridled enthusiasm. He or she is sure to shape things up, push people around differently, install some new systems, start building bridges with other managers, and generally try new things. If you can carry this mental exercise one more step, why not try to hold off your real-life termination by doing all those exciting new things your successor would do. Tell your boss you are looking to make your job more interesting—and more valuable to him—and ask him for his support and advice.

Summary thus far: The job you have usually has some value. If possible, try to:

1. Hold on to it.
2. Determine your underlying reasons for leaving.
3. Consider all your *options,* both inside and outside the company.

I'd be willing to wager that up to one half of the people who *can* stay, probably should; at least for 3 to 12 months more to test out some of these inside options.

Naturally, there are many valid reasons for leaving, from being fired, to taking advantage of an opportunity for professional or financial growth, to a recognition that you do want to make a basic career switch. Just make sure you know and understand your real reason.

A New Career?

Sometime between the ages of 20 and 65, you're bound to change your lifetime goals at least once, and perhaps not even know it. This gives you two life-shaking alternative problems:

1. You do recognize the change, but don't know what to do about it, or
2. You don't or won't (or can't) recognize the change in your goals.

The first problem is easier to address. This manual can help you find almost any kind of white-collar job. It's not a comprehensive career-counseling course, but for starters, go back and reread Chapter 3.

Unrecognized Change in Goals

However, if you are a manager, particularly at mid-life, you may not even recognize that you could be in the grips of Problem 2—the psychological shocker sometimes called mid-life crisis: "Where am I going? What's my life all about? What *do* I want to do with it now?" You can read a book such as *Passages* for some insight, but every case is different. Perhaps your spouse can serve as a sounding board or a mirror, and play back to you the changes he or she sees in you, and your latest apparent needs and life goals.

Furthermore, you are not immune to Problem 2 at any age, not even at 25 or 35! Following the Great American Success Story, you strive like a perpetual motion machine to fight your way to the top of the corporate ladder. You may have started a career at 20 in your chosen field or, more likely, started in a particular career path through sheer happenstance, and by your own ambition tried to windmill your way up. Your needs undoubtedly changed with time, and so did your related life-time goals. However, you diligently and unthinkingly kept on following the same path, propelled by your own momentum and by the pull of the American Way of Striving for Success in Your Career. Sometimes that can lead directly to case study I: From the frying pan into a very hot fire.

The Key Issue

The important point is that you may think that you have to make an immediate job change because of a career-path blockage or a personality conflict, when the real reason is hidden from you. You either have *not* thought it through all the way or have not considered your options, or else your basic career goals have changed. Thus, your general unhappiness may not be cured magically by a new boss or a new company.

There is no easy answer to this crisis, particularly if you don't recognize the underlying reason for your career unhappiness. Common sense tells us:

1. Don't automatically accept your old goals.
2. Don't accept the goals that supposedly have worked for the "successful" people you know, or see around you, in the business world.
3. Rather, try to determine what will make you happy on an ongoing, lifetime basis.
   (a) Perhaps you are in research but would much rather be in sales if you "had the chance."
   (b) Or, you work for Consolidated Multinational but would rather run your own woodworking business someday.
   (c) Or, you'd prefer to have a job with more (or perhaps, less) job stress and decision making.

(d)   Or, you'd rather have a staff position instead of being a direct-line supervisor.

(e)   Or, you may want to take some courses to see if you really *would* enjoy practicing law or accountancy.

This means forgetting your old ideas that "one more promotion or raise" will solve all your problems once and for all.

You've got to figure out, with the help of your spouse (or a qualified career consultant, if necessary), just what you *want* to do, and not what you think you should do. Don't be a shirker. Take responsibility for your life! Then you'll be able to make the necessary short- and long-term plans to allow you to finally do *your* own thing!

One more reminder: if you do know your real goals and still want to change jobs, go to it! Don't get too carried away by all this—none of it may pertain to you.

But, just in case it might apply, we think it is important to bring up. After all, there's no point in your changing jobs without knowing where you're going and why.

The Special Career Problems of Being Fired

Being fired is hard enough on your system at any age. It is worse when you are in the throes of a mid-life crisis. (Maybe you were fired *because* of your rudderless or emotional mid-life upheavals.)

But, whatever your age, don't jump for the first job you can get hold of on the rebound. The statistics say that you'll surely leave that one within a matter of a few short months, or maybe a year or so at the outside. And it may happen all over again if you rebound too quickly to still another job. That's much more common than you think.

Get with your spouse, your friends, or your closest advisers;

see if open and frank dialogue can help you understand that getting fired is obviously a big event. However, it's an ideal time to reevaluate your life and life goals, and to figure out what you want to do: a "lifetime-of-happiness" goal!

While you're at it, it's also a good time to steel up your courage and evaluate what you did wrong. Why were you fired in the first place (and also in the second or third places on the rebound, too)? Was it your own personal crisis, your political ineptness, or your basic disinterest in your chosen field?

Further, what were the purely circumstantial or outside or fate factors (such as a rapidly growing industry) and the self-caused factors (your lack of interest or training) that literally gave you success—or failure—during the various phases of your career? What sobering self-insight does that provide, particularly in terms of truly understanding your past track record and your future goals?

Taking a new job on a "rebound" is as bad as getting married for the same reason, and it has about the same chances of success. Spend the time to evaluate yourself and your life-goals. What could be more important than that, at any age?

T W E N T Y

REAL JOB INSURANCE

227

T he only ongoing job insurance policy you have is yourself. If you like your work, or (better yet) if you love it,
you are halfway to a permanent and paid-up job insurance policy. So, first:

1. Find a job and career that you enjoy.

The rest of your job security is a matter of:

2. Luck and timing
3. Your skills
4. Your ability to "Be Prepared" at all times.

Luck and Timing

Everyone has influence over all of these factors, even luck and
timing. Sure, these two depend heavily upon chance, but you
can help to increase the odds more in your favor. For example,
people who are optimistic and happy (with their jobs and
themselves) seem to effortlessly attract good luck, and good
timing too. These people are more than lucky: they make their
own opportunities because they have the confidence and optimism to do so.

Optimism allows you to make the very best of any situation—even a bad one—and that can't help but bring you luck.
Pessimists, on the other hand, endlessly carry around their
personalized and monogramed sets of bad luck plans that can
turn into self-fulfilling prophecies. They often may be jealous
of others or daydream of success, but possess a hidden, yet real
desire for failure.

So try to be both self-confident and optimistic. The two go
hand in hand, and are guaranteed to help you make your own
luck and lucky moves.

Your Skills

The next job security factor involves your three most important skills: managerial, technical, and personal. Both managerial and technical skills, it's now generally agreed, can be stud-
ied, practiced, learned, and refined.

Your ongoing premium payment on this type of job insurance is to study, practice, and hone these skills. Keep up with
new management techniques and technical advances: don't get
stale and fall into the rut of mechanical repetition. Always look
at your managerial and technical skills through a fresh eye,
and never stop investigating, studying, and practicing new
techniques.

If technical and managerial skills can be practiced and
learned, so can your personal skills. For example, you can
force yourself to give everyone a smile each morning—that's a
fine way to start a new habit or interpersonal skill. After a
while, your smile will be less forced. In fact, when you keep it
up you'll find (a) people smiling back; (b) you're doing it naturally, and not forced at all; (c) you'll get ahead faster, or at the
least, you'll have a better time in the meantime.

Be Prepared

The final clause in your job insurance policy is: Be Prepared.

If Lady Luck or the Genie of Good Timing keeps tapping
you on the shoulder, but you're not ready, you won't ever be
considered for a career opportunity. If you *are* ready, you can
take full advantage of these random opportunities, plus you
can also seek out your own good breaks.

Since job insurance includes not getting fired, or being ready
to get a new job quickly if the ax does fall, you'll need to prepare for that kind of "opportunity" as well.

How to Be Prepared for the Ax

First, of course, is to do a good job, keep your boss happy, and your skills honed. But you should *also* protect yourself from the Fast and Fickle Firing Finger of Fate by:

1. Keeping all your political fences mended throughout the company. Continually sniff the air, so you can catch the scent when the political winds change in your company.
2. Keep your ears open: stay current on what's happening in the job market.
3. Make sure you are clearly visible in the market, so that people throughout the industry know of you, and perhaps are even keeping an eye on you.

Some Tips on Political Preparation

These final tips apply to your current job, but are also very useful when starting a new job.

Visibility

1. Be a member of all the professional and industry societies, clubs, and associations that you possibly can.
2. Become active in a few of the above.
3. Volunteer for some committee work, particularly those with media coverage.
4. Give speeches.
5. Become an association officer.
6. Be sure to participate in both the business and social aspects of these groups.

7. Before, during, and after a job change, it is equally important to maintain all your contacts.

8. Write articles. One or two a year in a trade magazine can be a great help. Headhunters and competitors all read them. Don't forget to get reprints.

9. Have your job appointment announced in all the trade journals and newspapers that you possibly can. Have a professional photographer, not Uncle Burt, take your portrait, and get sufficient 8 x 10" glossy prints for all the media, since they won't return them.

Market Awareness

1. Keep up with industry events. (See the Visibility items.)

2. Read industry and trade publications, a big-city Sunday newspaper, *The Wall Street Journal, Fortune* or other business magazines, and professional journals.

3. Keep your resume up to date: periodically review your latest career objective, and recent accomplishments and projects.

4. Test the job-market waters: answer an occasional interesting ad. If an executive appointment is announced in an industry where you want to work, write to the new boss and offer your congratulations—and the opportunity to evaluate you in terms of Building His Own New Team.

On Your Current Job

1. Continue growing, improving your skills, and keeping up on industry politics.

2. Let your boss know that his goals are your goals.

3. Keep your boss up to date on what's happening, particularly on those projects or decisions that you have carried out or made. What you do reflects on him. He must know what you have (or haven't) been doing, and the direct implications on his own job security.

4. Run your staff so that it reflects well on you. Let them participate in the initial discussions on policies, major decisions, and setting of goals. The object is to get their input, consensus, enthusiasm, and loyalty.

5. Don't fall into the loser's trap of getting emotionally involved in office political wars. As the Law of Defensive Warfare warns:

    Watch your back:

    And defend or attack,

    With dispatch and ease

    But no overkill, please.

    (And don't get annoyed

    Or become paranoid).

    —It's only a game after all!

As we now have learned, society allows you to choose the members of your bowling team, but you have little or no choice of the office people you literally are forced to deal with. So, don't overreact to the gross injustice of working with people whose greatest asset is congenital stupidity.

No matter that these assorted fakes, flakes, knife-wielders, losers, slow learners, slackers, or lousy decision-makers populate your office. Welcome to the wonderful everyday world of human institutions and human beings. It's undoubtedly the same in every office on the face of the earth. So, live and let live, wherever you are, within the limits of self-defense given in this section.

Life is only a game after all, and being a winner is not difficult when you know how!

COMPANY MAILING LIST

Appendices 1 and 2 present the names and addresses of over 300 corporations and headhunters.
Warning: We have not included names of corporate officials, since these names do change. Turnover is common at every level, you see. Use your local library's reference books to get the latest names of the company officers you want to contact.

ABBOTT LABORATORIES
Abbott Park
North Chicago, IL 60064
(312) 688-6100

ALBERTO-CULVER
COMPANY
2525 W. Armitage Avenue
Melrose Park, IL 60160
(312) 450-3000

ALMAY, INC.
850 Third Avenue
New York, NY 10022
(212) 888-1990

ALLEGHENY INTERNATIONAL
INC.
Two Oliver Building
Pittsburgh, PA 15222
(412) 562-4000

ALLIED CORPORATION
Box 2245R
Morristown, NJ 07960
(201) 455-2000

ALLIED STORES CORPORATION
1114 Avenue of the Americas
New York, NY 10036
(212) 764-2000

ALLIS-CHALMERS
CORPORATION
1205 South 70 Street
West Allis, WI 53214

ALUMINUM CO. OF AMERICA
1501 Alcoa Building
Pittsburgh, PA 15219
(412) 553-4707

AMERICAN AIRLINES, INC.
P.O. Box 61616
Dallas/Fort Worth Airport
TX 75261
(214) 355-1234

ARMOUR-DIAL COMPANY
Division of Greyhound
   Corporation
111 W. Clarendon
Phoenix, AZ 85077
(602) 248-5176

AMERICAN BRANDS, INC.
245 Park Avenue
New York, NY 10017
(212) 557-7000

AMERICAN CAN COMPANY
American Lane
Greenwich, CT 06830
(203) 552-2000

AMERICAN CYANAMID
COMPANY
Wayne, NJ 07470
(201) 831-1234

AMERICAN EXPRESS
COMPANY
American Express Plaza
New York, NY 10004
(212) 323-2000

AMERICAN HOSPITAL SUPPLY
CORP.
One American Plaza
Evanston, IL 60201
(312) 866-4000

AMERICAN STANDARD INC.
40 West 40 Street
New York, NY 10018
(212) 840-5100

AMERICAN STORES COMPANY
P.O. Box 27447
709 East South Temple
Salt Lake City, UT 84127
(801) 539-0112

AMERICAN TELEPHONE AND
TELEGRAPH COMPANY
195 Broadway
New York, NY 10007
(212) 393-9800

AFM INCORPORATED
777 Westchester Avenue
White Plains, NY 10604
(914) 694-9000

ARA SERVICES, INC.
Philadelphia, PA 19106
(215) 574-5000

ASHLAND OIL, INC.
1401 Winchester Avenue
Ashland, KY 41101
(606) 329-3333

AMWAY CORPORATION
7575 E. Fulton Road
Ada, MI 49301
(616) 676-6000

ATLANTIC RICHFIELD
COMPANY
515 S. Flower Street
Los Angeles, CA 90071
(213) 486-3511

AUTOMATIC DATA
PROCESSING, INC.
405 Route 3
Clifton, NJ 07015
(201) 365-7300

AVCO CORPORATION
1275 King Street
Greenwich, CT 68030
(203) 552-1800

AVON PRODUCTS, INC.
9 West 57 Street
New York, NY 10019
(212) 593-4017

C.R. BARD, INC.
731 Central Avenue
Murray Hill, NJ 07974
(201) 277-8000

BEATRICE FOODS COMPANY
2 N. LaSalle Street
Chicago, IL 60602
(312) 782-3820

BORDEN, INC.
277 Park Avenue
New York, NY 10172
(212) 573-4000

BRISTOL-MEYERS COMPANY
345 Park Avenue
New York, NY 10154
(212) 644-2100

BURLINGTON INDUSTRIES,
INC.
3330 W. Friendly Avenue
Greensboro, NC 27420
(919) 379-2000

BURROUGHS CORPORATION
Detroit, MI 48232
(313) 972-7000

BURROUGHS WELLCOME CO.
3030 Cornwallis Road
Research Triangle Park
Durham, NC 27709
(919) 541-9090

CARTER-WALLACE, INC.
767 Fifth Avenue
New York, NY 10022
(212) 758-4500

CATERPILLAR TRACTOR
COMPANY
100 N.E. Adams Street
Peoria, IL 61629
(309) 675-1000

CBS INCORPORATED
51 West 52 Street
New York, NY 10019
(212) 975-6075

CHARLES OF THE RITZ
GROUP, LTD.
Division of Squibb Corp.
40 W. 57 Street
New York, NY 10019
(212) 621-7327

CENTRAL SOYA COMPANY
1300 Fort Wayne
Fort Wayne, IN 46802
(219) 425-5700

CHESEBROUGH-PONDS
33 Benedict Place
Greenwich, CT 06830
(203) 661-2000

CHANEL
9 West 57 Street
New York, NY 10019
(212) 688-5055

THE CLOROX COMPANY
1221 Broadway
Oakland, CA 94612
(415) 271-7000

COLGATE-PALMOLIVE
COMPANY
300 Park Avenue
New York, NY 10022
(212) 751-1200

CONSOLIDATED FOODS
CORPORATION
135 S. LaSalle Street
Chicago, IL 60603
(312) 726-6414

CONTROL DATA
CORPORATION
8100 34 Avenue South
Minneapolis, MN 55420
(612) 853-8100

COSMAIR, INC.
530 Fifth Avenue
New York, NY 10036
(212) 840-3900

CPC INTERNATIONAL, INC.
Englewood Cliffs, NJ 07632
(201) 894-4000

DART & KRAFT, INC.
Glenview, IL 60025
(312) 998-2000

DEERE & COMPANY
Moline, IL 61265
(309) 752-8000

DENTSPLY INTERNATIONAL
INC.
570 W. College Avenue
York, PA 17405
(717) 845-7511

DeSoto Chemical Co., Inc.
P.O. Box 70
Arcadia, FL 33821
(813) 494-3232

Dormar Chemicals Inc.
44 Lewis Street
Paterson, NJ 07501
(201) 345-6780

Dow Chemical Company
2030 Dow Center
Midland, MI 48640
(517) 636-1000

Eastman Kodak Company
343 State Street
Rochester, NY 14650
(716) 724-4000

Economics Laboratory,
  Inc.
Osborn Building
St. Paul, MN 55102
(612) 224-4678

Engelhard Corporation
Menlo Park, NJ 08810
(201) 321-5000

Esmark, Inc.
55 E. Monroe Street
Chicago, IL 60603
(312) 431-3600

Exxon Corporation
1251 Avenue of the Americas
New York, NY 10020
(212) 398-3093

Faberge, Inc.
1345 Avenue of the Americas
New York, NY 10019

Fairchild Idustries, Inc.
20301 Century Boulevard
Germantown, MD 20767

Federal Paper Board
  Company, Inc.
75 Chestnut Ridge Road
Montvale, NJ 07645

Firestone Tire and
  Rubber Company
1200 Firestone Parkway
Akron, OH 44317
(216) 379-7000

Fluor Corporation
3333 Michelson Drive
Irvine, CA 92730

FMC Corporation
200 East Randolph Drive
Chicago, IL 60601
(312) 861-6000

Foremost-McKesson, Inc.
One Post Street
San Francisco, CA 94104
(415) 983-8300

General Dynamics
  Corporation
Pierre Laclede Center
St. Louis, MO 63105
(314) 862-2400

GENERAL ELECTRIC
COMPANY
3135 Easton Turnpike
Fairfield, CT 06431
(203) 373-2431

GENERAL FOODS
CORPORATION
250 North Street
White Plains, NY 10625
(914) 683-2500

GENERAL TELEPHONE &
ELECTRONICS CORPORA-
TION
One Stamford Forum
Stamford, CT 06904
(203) 357-2000

GETTY OIL COMPANY
3810 Wilshire Boulevard
Los Angeles, CA 90010
(213) 381-7151

GILLETTE COMPANY
Prudential Tower Building
Boston, MA 02199
(617) 421-7000

W.R. GRACE & CO.
1114 Avenue of the Americas
New York, NY 10036
(212) 764-5555

GREYHOUND CORPORATION
Greyhound Tower
Phoenix, AZ 85077
(602) 248-4000

GULF & WESTERN
INDUSTRIES, INC.
1 Gulf & Western Plaza
New York, NY 10023
(212) 333-7000

HERCULES, INC.
910 Market Street
Wilmington, DE 19899
(302) 575-5000

HEUBLEIN, INC.
Munson Road
Farmington, CT 06032
(203) 677-4061

HOOVER COMPANY
101 Maple Street
North Canton, OH 44720
(216) 499-9200

INTERNATIONAL BUSINESS
MACHINES CORP.
Armonk, NY 10504
(914) 756-1900

INSILCO CORPORATION
1000 Research Parkway
Meriden, CT 06450
(203) 634-2000

INTERNATIONAL PAPER
COMPANY
77 West 45 Street
New York, NY 10036
(212) 223-1268

INTERNATIONAL TELEPHONE
& TELEGRAPH CORPORA-
TION
320 Park Avenue
New York, NY 10022
(212) 752-6000

INMONT CORPORATION
1255 Broad Street
Clifton, NJ 07015
(201) 365-3400

INTERPACE CORPORATION
260 Cherry Hill Road
Parsippany, NJ 07054
(201) 335-1111

J. M. CORPORATION
P.O. Box 5108
Ken-Caryl Ranch
Denver, CO 80217
(303) 979-1000

KIDDE INC.
9 Brighton Road
Clifton, NJ 07015
(201) 777-6500

KOPPERS CORPORATION, INC.
Pittsburgh, PA 15219
(412) 227-2000

KROGER COMPANY
1014 Vine Street
Cincinnati, OH 45201
(513) 762-4000

LEAR SIEGLER, INC.
3171 South Bundy Drive
Santa Monica, CA 90406
(213) 391-7211

LENOX INC.
Old Princeton Pike
Lawrenceville, NJ 08648
(609) 896-2800

LEVER BROTHERS COMPANY
390 Park Avenue
New York, NY 10022
(212) 688-6000

MARY KAY COSMETICS, INC.
8787 Stemmon Freeway
Dallas, TX 75247
(214) 630-8787

MATTEL, INC.
5150 Rosecrans Avenue
Hawthorne, CA 90250
(213) 644-6411

MERCK & CO., INC.
P.O. Box 2000
Rahway, NJ 07065

MOBIL CORPORATION
150 East 42 Street
New York, NY 10017
(212) 883-4242

MOTOROLA, INC.
1303 East Algonquin Road
Schaumburg, IL 60196
(312) 397-5000

NABISCO BRANDS, INC.
East Hanover, NJ 07936
(201) 884-0500

NORTON SIMON, INC.
277 Park Avenue
New York, NY 10017
(212) 832-1000

PENNWALT CORPORATION
Three Parkway
Philadelphia, PA 19102
(215) 587-7320

PFIZER INC.
235 East 42 Street
New York, NY 10017
(212) 573-2323

PUROLATOR, INC.
255 Old New Brunswick
  Road
Piscataway, NJ 08854
(201) 885-1100

ROYCE-CHEMICAL CO.
17 Carlton Avenue
East Rutherford, NJ 07073

RHONE-POULENC CHEMICAL
  CO.
P.O. Box 125
Monmouth Junction, NJ
  08852
(201) 297-0100

RORER GROUP INC.
500 Virginia Drive
Fort Washington, PA 19034
(215) 628-6000

SAFEWAY STORES, INC.
Fourth & Jackson Streets
Oakland, CA 94660
(415) 891-3000

SCHERING-PLOUGH
  CORPORATION
Galloping Hill Road
Kenilworth, NJ 07033
(201) 931-2000

SCOTT PAPER COMPANY
Scott Plaza
Philadelphia, PA 19113
(215) 521-5000

SMITHKLINE CORPORATION
One Franklin Plaza
Philadelphia, PA 19010
(215) 854-4000

SQUIBB CORPORATION
40 West 57 Street
New York, NY 10019
(212) 621-7000

STERLING DRUG
  INCORPORATED
90 Park Avenue
New York, NY 10016
(212) 972-4141

SUPERMARKETS GENERAL
  CORP.
301 Blair Road
Woodbridge, NJ 07095
(201) 499-3000

TIME INCORPORATED
Time & Life Building
New York, NY 10020
(212) 586-1212

TOYS "R" US
395 West Passaic Street
Rochelle Park, NJ 07662
(201) 845-5033

THE TRANE COMPANY
3600 Pammel Creek Road
La Crosse, WI 54601
(608) 787-2000

UNION CAMP CORPORATION
1600 Valley Road
Wayne, NJ 07470
(201) 628-9000

UNION CARBIDE
CORPORATION
270 Park Avenue
New York, NY 10017
(212) 551-2345

WARNER-LAMBERT
COMPANY
201 Tabor Road
Morris Plains, NJ 07950
(201) 540-2000

WEST CHEMICAL
PRODUCTS, INC.
1000 Herrontown Road
Princeton, NJ 08540
(609) 921-0501

WHITTAKER, CLARK
& DANIELS, INC.
1000 Coolidge Street
So. Plainfield, NJ 07080
(201) 561-6100

J.B. WILLIAMS CO.
East Hanover, NJ 07936
(201) 884-0500

WITCO CHEMICAL CORP.
277 Park Avenue
New York, NY 10017
(212) 872-4200

XEROX CORPORATION
Stamford, CT 06904
(203) 329-8700

ZURN INDUSTRIES, INC.
One Zurn Place
Erie, PA 16512
(814) 452-2111

EXECUTIVE RECRUITER LIST

Warning: Turnover (or new addresses) affects the accuracy of any mailing list. (For a complete and updated directory see the Reference given at the beginning of Chapter 12.)

AD-TECH PERSONNEL
1144 Clifton Avenue
Clifton, NJ 07013

AHRENS, DAVIS &
  ASSOCIATES, INC.
20 Tower Lane
Avon, CT 06001

GENE ALAN ASSOCIATES
625 Main Avenue
Passaic, NJ 07055

F.A. ALRICH & ASSOCIATES
37 Station Drive
Princeton Junction,
  NJ 08550

AMANSCO, INC.
100 Fifth Avenue Building
Pittsburgh, PA 15222

THE ANDRE-DREW CORP.
Suite 845
Valley Forge Plaza
King of Prussia, PA 19406

ANTELL, NAGEL, MOORHEAD
  & ASSOC.
230 Park Avenue
New York, NY 10017

R.W. APPLE & ASSOCIATES
200 Atlantic Avenue
Manasquan, NJ 08736

WILLIAM B. ARNOLD &
ASSOC.
1776 S. Jackson Street
Denver, CO 80210

ARTHUR PERSONNEL
Suite 100
8 Forest Avenue
Caldwell, NJ 07006

BALLOS & CO., INC.
415 Speedwell Avenue
Morris Plains, NJ 07950

BARONE O'HARA
ASSOCIATES
29 Emmons Drive
Princeton, NJ 08540

NATHAN BARRY ASSOCIATES,
INC.
301 Union Wharf
Boston, MA 02109

BARTHOLDI & CO, INC.
65 William Street
Wellesley Hills, MA 02181

BARTON-SANS
551 Fifth Avenue
New York, NY 10017

E.C. BATKIN ASSOCIATES,
INC.
Box 2158
Teaneck, NJ 07666

BATTALIA, LOTZ, &
ASSOCIATES
342 Madison Avenue
New York, NY 10017

J.W. BAUDER ASSOCIATES
Suite 280
16475 Dallas Parkway
Dallas, TX 75248

MARTIN H. BAUMAN
ASSOCIATES
410 Park Avenue
New York, NY 10022

GARY S. BELL ASSOCIATES,
INC.
393 Crescent Avenue
Wyckoff, NJ 07481

BENTLEY & EVANS, INC.
1 Penn Plaza
New York, NY 10019

C. BERKE & ASSOCIATES
3131 Princeton Pike
Lawrenceville, NJ 08648

BERNDTSON INTERNATIONAL
551 Fifth Avenue
New York, NY 10036

BESEN ASSOCIATES
16–18 Washington Street
Morristown, NJ 07960

BILLINGTON, FOX & ELLIS
20 North Wacker Drive
Chicago, IL 60606

BINARY SEARCH
2517 Route 35
Manasquan, NJ 08736

BLAU, KAPTAIN & ASSOC.
R.D. 4
Box 447D
North Brunswick, NJ 08903

BLENDOW, CROWLEY &
OLIVER, INC.
420 Lexington Avenue
New York, NY 10017

MARC-PAUL BLOOME LTD.
250 West 57 Street
New York, NY 10007

JOHN C. BOONE & CO.
19505 Warwick Drive
Brookfield, WI 53005

BOWDEN & CO.
5000 Rockside Road
Suite 120
Cleveland, OH 44131

BOYDEN ASSOCIATES, INC.
260 Madison Avenue
New York, NY 10016

BREITMAYER ASSOCIATES
72 Park Street
New Canaan, CT 06840

BRENNAN ASSOCIATES
Box 947
F.D.R. Station
New York, NY 10022

BRENTWOOD PERSONNEL
ASSOC.
1280 Route 46
Box 11E
Parsippany, NJ 07054

D.A.K. BROWN &
ASSOCIATES, INC.
420 Lexington Avenue
New York, NY 10017

BRJ ASSOCIATES
1590 East 2 Street
Scotch Plains, NJ 07076

BROOKS/GAY & ASSOCIATES
50 Park Avenue
New York, NY 10016

THOMAS A. BUFFUM
ASSOCIATES
2 Century Plaza
Boston, MA 02108

BURKE & O'BRIEN
ASSOCIATES, INC.
233 Broadway
New York, NY 10007

E.A. BUTLER & ASSOCIATES
1270 Avenue of the Americas
New York, NY 10020

CADILLAC ASSOCIATES, INC.
32 West Randolph Street
Chicago, IL 60601

CANNY, BOWEN INC.
425 Park Avenue
New York, NY 10022

CAPRIO & ASSOCIATES, INC.
2625 Butterfield Road
Oak Brook, IL 60521

CARRIS, JACKOWITZ ASSOC.
201 East 79 Street
New York, NY 10021

DAVIS CHAMBERS &
ASSOCIATES
6 East 43 Street
New York, NY 10017

CHERBONNIER & PEBWORTH
445 N. Post Oak Lane
Houston, TX 77024

CHRISTENSON &
MONTGOMERY, INC.
250 Madison Avenue
Morristown, NJ 07960

WILLIAM H. CLARK &
ASSOCIATES
330 Madison Avenue
New York, NY 10017

CLAYMORE ASSOCIATES
274 Madison Avenue
New York, NY 10016

STEPHEN D. COINE &
ASSOCIATES
250 Post Road E.
Westport, CT 06880

JOSEPH CONLEY &
ASSOCIATES
122 East 42 Street
New York, NY 10017

COOPERS & LYBRAND
1000 W. 6 Street
Los Angeles, CA 90017

CORDANE ASSOCIATES, INC.
250 Madison Avenue
Morristown, NJ 07960

CORRY, HOWE ASSOCIATES,
INC.
Time & Life Building
New York, NY 10020

ALLAN COX & ASSOCIATES
410 N. Michigan Avenue
Chicago, IL 60611

LEE CRIPPIN, INC.
9300 W. 110 Street
Overland Park, KS 66210

CRIS ASSOCIATES INC.
274 Madison Avenue
New York, NY 10016

CURRY, TELLERI, ZIEGLER,
INC.
Route 27 & Parsonage Road
Menlo Park, NJ 08820

THORNDIKE DELAND
ASSOCIATES
1440 Broadway
New York, NY 10018

DEMERLIER, REYNOLDS,
RETTIG & ASSOCIATES
617 S. Olive Street, Suite
1000
Los Angeles, CA 90014

DENNY & CO., INC.
3 Gateway Center
Pittsburgh, PA 15222

HAROLD DENTON
ASSOCIATES
3 Girald Plaza, Suite 1320
Philadelphia, PA 19102

DeVoto & Benz Partners
120 S. Riverside Pl.
Chicago, IL 60606

Jack Dill Associates
777 Third Avenue
New York, NY 10017

Donworth, Taylor
  Associates
1111 Third Avenue
Seattle, WA 98101

Dunhill Personnel
  System
1 Old Country Road
Carle Place, NY 11803

Eastern Executive
  Association
881 Allwood Road
Clifton, NJ 07012

Eastman & Beaudine, Inc.
111 W. Monroe Street
Chicago, IL 60603

Einstein Associates
380 Lexington Avenue
New York, NY 10007

Ernst & Whinney
Executive Search Division
2000 National City Center
Cleveland, OH 44115

Henry H. Eskay
24 Hutton Avenue
West Orange, NJ 07052

Evans Associates
44 Montgomery Street
San Francisco, CA 94104

Walth Evers & Co.
13515 Shaker Boulevard
Cleveland, OH 44120

Terrence N. Flanagan
  Assoc.
222 Martling Avenue,
  Apt. 4D
Tarrytown, NY 10591

Folger & Co., Ltd.
214 Lewis Wharf
Boston, MA 02110

Forest Associates
8 Forest Avenue
Caldwell, NJ 07006

George W. Fotis &
  Associates
170 Mason Street
Greenwich, CT 06830

Fox-Morris Associates
1500 Chestnut Street
Philadelphia, PA 19102

Fry Consultants, Inc.
1 Park Place
Suite 450
Atlanta, GA 30318

General Search
  Associates
555 Fifth Avenue
New York, NY 10017

N.W. GIBSON ASSOC., INC.
5900 Wilshire Boulevard
Suite 760
Los Angeles, CA 90036

J.B. GILBERT ASSOCIATES,
  INC.
420 Lexington Avenue
New York, NY 10017

GILBERT TWEED & ASSOC.,
  INC.
630 Third Avenue
New York, NY 10017

GILMORE PERSONNEL
  CONSULTANTS
589 Franklin Turnpike
Ridgewood, NJ 07450

ALAN GLOU ASSOCIATES
400 Hunnewell Avenue
Needham, MA 02192

GOLIGHTLY & CO.,
  INTERNATIONAL
1 Rockefeller Plaza
New York, NY 10020

THE GOODRICH &
  SHERWOOD CO.
521 Fifth Avenue
New York, NY 10017

GOULD & McCOY, INC.
375 Park Avenue
New York, NY 10017

GRAHAM ASSOCIATES
111 Madison Avenue
Morristown, NJ 07960

HALBRECHT ASSOCIATES,
  INC.
1200 Sumner Street
Stamford, CT 06905

HALEY ASSOCIATES, INC.
375 Park Avenue
New York, NY 10015

HANDY ASSOCIATES, INC.
245 Park Avenue
New York, NY 10022

HANSEN & KIRKPATRICK
1136 Union Mall
Honolulu, Hawaii 96813

HANZEL, WACHTER &
  ASSOCIATES
310 Madison Avenue
New York, NY 10017

HARRIS & U'REN, INC.
1976 Arizona Bank Building
Phoenix, AZ 85003

HASKELL & STERN
  ASSOCIATES
529 Fifth Avenue
New York, NY 10017

D.P. HEALEY & ASSOCIATES
200 Atlantic Avenue
Manasquan, NJ 08736

F.P. HEALY & CO.
630 Third Avenue
New York, NY 10017

ROBERT HELDRICK
ASSOCIATES
20 N. Wacker Drive
Chicago, IL 60606

HEIDRICK & STRUGGLES,
INC.
125 S. Wacker Drive
Chicago, IL 60606

ROBERT HELLER ASSOCIATES,
INC.
25 Valley Drive
Greenwich, CT 06830

HELMICH, MILLER & PASEK,
INC.
5725 E. River Road
Chicago, IL 60631

HERGENRATHER & CO.
3435 Wilshire Boulevard
Los Angeles, CT 90010

HIRSCH & ASSOCIATES
1 Stockade Road
Warren, NJ 07060

HODGE-CRONIN &
ASSOCIATES
9575 W. Higgins Road
Rosemont, IL 60018

HOUZE, SHOURDS &
MONTGOMERY
2029 Century Park East
Los Angeles, CA 90067

ROBERT HOWE &
ASSOCIATES
2971 Flower Road South
Atlanta, GA 30341

WARD HOWELL
INTERNATIONAL, INC.
99 Park Avenue
New York, NY 10016

HUMAN RESOURCE SERVICES
230 Park Avenue
New York, NY 10017

THE HUNT COMPANY
274 Madison Avenue
New York, NY 10016

INSIDE MANAGEMENT
ASSOCIATES
143 East 35 Street
New York, NY 10016

INTERNATIONAL MANAGE-
MENT ADVISORS, INC.
485 Lexington Avenue
New York, NY 10017

CHARLES IRISH
420 Lexington Avenue
New York, NY 10017

HAROLD C. JOHNSON & CO.
1550 Spring Road
Oak Brook, IL 60521

JONAS & ASSOCIATES, INC.
333 N. Mayfair Road
Milwaukee, WI 53222

KAHLERT ASSOCIATES, INC.
375 Park Avenue
New York, NY 10022

THE KEARNY COMPANY
Executive Search Division
222 S. Riverside Plaza
Chicago, IL 60606

KEATING, GRIMM & LEEPER,
  INC.
717 Fifth Avenue
New York, NY 10022

KENSINGTON EXECUTIVE
  SEARCH
25 Third Street
Stamford, CT 06905

JOSEPH KEYES ASSOCIATES
354 State Street
Hackensack, NJ 07601

KEYTON ASSOCIATES
387 Springfield Avenue
Summit, NJ 07901

KORN/FERRY
  INTERNATIONAL
277 Park Avenue
New York, NY 10017

KREMPLE & MEADE
1900 Avenue of the Stars
Los Angeles, CA 90067

KROW ASSOCIATES
7 Glenwood Avenue
East Orange, NJ 07017

KUNZER ASSOC., LTD.
208 S. LaSalle Street
Chicago, IL 60604

LOR ASSOCIATES
1101 State Road
Princeton, NJ 08540

LACROSSE ASSOCIATES
1600 Route 22
Union, NJ 07083

LAMALLE ASSOCIATES, INC.
13920 N. Dale Mabry
Tampa, FL 33618

BRECK LARDNER ASSOC.,
  INC.
Box 611
Essex, CT 06426

LAUER, SBARBARO
  ASSOCIATES
1 N. LaSalle Street
Chicago, IL 60602

LAWRENCE-LEITH & CO.
427 West 12 Street
Kansas City, MO 64105

HENRY LEONARD
  ASSOCIATES
Box 3896
New York, NY 10017

LOCKE & ASSOCIATES
3145 NCNB Plaza
Charlotte, NC 28280

FRANK LOCKETT ASSOCIATES
818 Olive Street
Suite 762
St. Louis, MO 63101

ARTHUR J. LOVELEY
ASSOCIATES
60 East 42 Street
New York, NY 10016

FRED LUSTIG & ASSOCIATES
12903 Copperstone Drive
Sun City West, AZ 85375

ROBERT MADIGAN ASSOC.,
INC.
110 East 42 Street
New York, NY 10017

MAGLIO & CO.
16535 Bluemound Road
Brookfield, WI 53003

MANAGEMENT ADVISORS OF
PRINCETON
228 Alexander Street
Princeton, NY 08540

MANAGEMENT RECRUITERS
INTERNATIONAL
1015 Euclid Avenue
Cleveland, OH 44115

MANAGEMENT SEARCH, INC.
621 S.W. Morrison Street
Portland, OR 97205

MARC ASSOCIATES, INC.
B-124 Park Drive Manor
Philadelphia, PA 19144

MASSEY, CHARBONNEAU,
TRAPNELL, INC.
1115 Sherbrooke Street W.
Montreal, Quebec
H3A 1H3 Canada

MCBRIDE ASSOCIATES, INC.
1511 K Street NW
Washington, DC 20005

EDWIN MCDONALD
ASSOCIATES
341 Madison Avenue
New York, NY 10017

MCFEELY, WACKERLE
ASSOCIATES
20 No. Wacker Drive
Chicago, IL 60606

MEEHAN ASSOCIATES
3380 Monroe Avenue
Rochester, NY 14618

MARTIN H. MEISEL
ASSOCIATES
55 East 87 Street
New York, NY 10028

MINTON & ASSOCIATES, INC.
1670 Broadway
Denver, CO 80202

MORIARTY/FOX, INC.
20 N. Wacker Drive
Chicago, IL 60606

MSL INTERNATIONAL
CONSULTANTS, LTD.
1 Dag Hammarskjold Plaza
New York, NY 10017

MWS SEARCH CONSULTANTS
55 E. Monroe Street
Suite 4314
Chicago, IL 60603

NEWELL, DOUCETTE &
ASSOCIATES
30 East 40 Street
New York, NY 10016

NEW ENGLAND RECRUITERS
900 Chapel Street
New Haven, CT 06510

PAUL NUMEROF ASSOCIATES
10 Ryan Road
Edison, NJ 08817

NADZAM, LUSK &
ASSOCIATES
3211 Scott Boulevard
Santa Clara, CA 95051

F.M. O'GRADY & ASSOC.
22 Angus Lane
Warren, NJ 07060

OLIVER & ROZNER
ASSOCIATES, INC.
598 Madison Avenue
New York, NY 10022

O'NEIL EXECUTIVE SEARCH
P.O. Box 135
Buffalo, NY 14223

ORGANIZATION RESOURCES,
INC.
63 Atlantic Avenue
Boston, MA 02110

OWEN, WEBB, BACCI,
BENNETT, INC.
280 Park Avenue
New York, NY 10017

P.A.R. ASSOCIATES
27 State Street
Boston, MA 02109

PA INTERNATIONAL
MANAGEMENT CONSUL-
TANTS
200 Park Avenue
New York, NY 10017

JOHN PAISIOS & ASSOCIATES
2222 Kensington Court
Oak Brook, IL 60521

PARENTI & JACOBS, INC.
115 S. LaSalle Street
Chicago, IL 60603

PARKER, ELDRIDGE, SHOLL
& GORDON
440 Tottin Pond Road
Waltham, MA 02154

PARMENTER ASSOCIATES
555 Madison Avenue
New York, NY 10022

PASCAL ASSOCIATES, INC.
82 Park Avenue
Rutherford, NJ 07070

BRUCE PAYNE CONSULTANTS,
INC.
666 Fifth Avenue
New York, NY 10019

PEAT, MARWICK, MITCHELL
& CO.
Executive Search Division
303 E. Wacker Drive
Chicago, IL 60601

THE PERSONNEL
LABORATORY
733 Sumner Street
Stamford, CT 06901

PIERCE & ASSOCIATES
American Bank Tower
Austin, TX 78701

PINSKER & SHATTUCK, INC.
14375 Saratoga Avenue
Saratoga, CA 95070

RENE PLESSNER ASSOCIATES,
INC.
450 Park Avenue
New York, NY 10022

POULOS ASSOCIATES
1139 Scott Avenue
Winnetka, IL 60093

EUGENE C. PRESSLER
Box 132
Blue Bell, PA 19422

HARRY J. PRIOR &
ASSOCIATES
700 112 Avenue NE
Belleville, WA 98004

RATH & STRONG, INC.
21 Worthen Road
Lexington, MA 02173

PAUL R. RAY & CO., INC.
277 Park Avenue
New York, NY 10017

REESE ASSOCIATES
135 Cumberland Road
Pittsburgh, PA 15237

RUSSELL REYNOLDS ASSOC.,
INC.
245 Park Avenue
New York, NY 10017

K.J. RICKLIN
505 Fifth Avenue
New York, NY 10017

ROBISON, SOCKWELL &
MCAULAY
3100 NCNB Plaza
Charlotte, NC 28280

ROCHE ASSOCIATES
Box 1353
Stamford, CT 06904

ROGERS, SLADE & HILL, INC.
17 Wilmont Lane
Riverside, CT 06878

LOUIS RUDZINSKY
ASSOCIATES
1656 Massachusetts Avenue
Lexington, MA 02173

SALES CONSULTANTS
INTERNATIONAL
1015 Euclid Avenue
Cleveland, OH 44115

SALES RECRUITERS
332 S. Michigan Avenue
Chicago, IL 60604

SALES & MANAGEMENT
SEARCH, INC.
120 S. Riverside Drive
Chicago, IL 60606

SCHNEIDER, HILL &
ASSOCIATES
710 Western Savings Bank
Building
Philadelphia, PA 19107

F.R. SCHWAB & ASSOCIATES,
INC.
645 Madison Avenue
New York, NY 10022

SCHWARZKOPF
CONSULTANTS, INC.
15285 Watertown Plank
Road
Elm Grove, WI 53122

SELECT SEARCH
7600 Parklawn Avenue S.
Minneapolis, MI 55435

JOHN W. SILER &
ASSOCIATES, INC.
5261 Port Washington
Road N.
Milwaukee, WI 53217

D.A. SILVERSTEIN
ASSOCIATES
375 Park Avenue
New York, NY 10022

SKOTT/EDWARDS
CONSULTANTS, INC.
250 Park Avenue
New York, NY 10017

EDWIN B. SINGER & CO.
One Penn Plaza
Suite 100
New York, NY 10001

SPRIGGS & CO., INC.
John Hancock Center
Suite 4015
Chicago, IL 60611

WILLIAM STACK ASSOCIATES,
INC.
230 Park Avenue
New York, NY 10017

PAUL SAFFORD ASSOCIATES,
LTD.
45 Rockefeller Plaza
New York, NY 10011

STAUB, WARMBOLD &
ASSOCIATES
655 Third Avenue
New York, NY 10017

STURM, BURROWS & CO.
1420 Walnut Street
Philadelphia, PA 19102

S.K. STEWART & ASSOCIATES
Executive Building
Box 40110
Cincinnati, OH 45240

ALLAN STOLEE PARTNERS,
INC.
110 Bloor Street W.
Suite 300
Toronto, Ontario M5S 2W7
Canada

SPENCER STUART &
ASSOCIATES
500 N. Michigan Avenue
Chicago, IL 60611

SPENCER STUART &
ASSOCIATES
4720 First International
Plaza
Houston, TX 77002

STUART-MILLS ASSOCIATES
311 S. Washington Street
Box 288
Alexandria, VA 22314

SUCCESSFUL WOMAN, INC.
1722 Connecticut Avenue,
NW
Washington, DC 20009

TORRETTO & ASSOCIATES,
INC.
Box 265—307 Bridgeway
Sausalito, CA 94965

TOUCHE ROSS & CIE
1 Place Ville Marie
Suite 2220
Montreal, Quebec
H3B 2A2 Canada

UPTON MANAGEMENT
SERVICE, INC.
2000 W. Big Beaver Road
Suite 208
Troy, MI 48084

JAMES WALKER ASSOCIATES,
INC.
702 Lincoln Federal Building
Louisville, KY 40202

WALTERS & CO.
4418 Davidson Avenue
Atlanta, GA 30319

WALLINGER ASSOCIATES
12–16 Bank Street
Summit, NJ 07901

HILTON N. WASSERMAN &
ASSOC.
200 Park Avenue
New York, NY 10017

WORDEN & RISBERG, INC.
1234 Market Street E.
Philadelphia, PA 19107

WOMAN EXEC, INC.
Box 938
Orinda, CA 94563

XAVIER ASSOCIATES, INC.
850 Rear Providence Way
Dedham, MA 02026

RESUME WORKSHEETS

OBJECTIVE

The position I seek is: _____

_____

Amount of responsibility: _____

_____

_____

In a company that is: _____

Character of company: _____

_____

_____

Size: _____

_____

Industry: _____

_____

Products: _____

_____

_____

_____

Location: _____

_____

_____

Travel?: _____

_____

_____

Relocate?: _____

_____

_____

PERSONAL DATA

Name: _____

Address: _____

Telephone No.: _____

Height: _____ Weight: _____

Other:_____

Language fluency (read, write, speak): _____

PRESENT OR LAST POSITION

Company name: _____

Division name: _____

Job title: _____

Report to (job title): _____

Dates: Start: _____ To: _____

Responsibilities: _____

_____

_____

_____

_____

_____

List 10 major accomplishments (use concrete/quantified dollars, number of products involved, etc., and action words: "reduced, achieved, created, sold, designed, implemented" are grabbing sentence starters.)

1. _____

_____

2. _____

_____

3. _____

_____

4. _____

_____

5. _____

_____

6. _____

_____

7. _____

_____

8. _____

_____

9. _____

_____

10. _____

_____

Other (promotions, salary increases, transfers, new titles, etc.):

_____

_____

_____

_____

_____

_____

Major decisions, recommendations adopted by company: _____

_____

_____

_____

_____

_____

_____

_____

_____

_____

_____

FIRST PRIOR EMPLOYER

Company name: _____

Division name: _____

Job title: _____

Report to (job title): _____

Dates: Start: _____ To: _____

Responsibilities: _____

_____

_____

_____

_____

List 6 major accomplishments (use concrete/quantified dollars, number of products involved, etc., and action words: "reduced, achieved, created, sold, designed, implemented" are grabbing sentence starters.)

1. _____

_____

2. _____

_____

3. _____

_____

4. _____

_____

5. _____

_____

6. _____

_____

Other (promotions, salary increases, transfers, new titles, etc.):

_____

_____

_____

_____

_____

Major decisions, recommendations adopted by company:

_____

_____

_____

_____

_____

_____

_____

_____

_____

SECOND PRIOR EMPLOYER

Company name: _____

Division name: _____

Job title: _____

Report to (job title): _____

Dates: Start: _____ To: _____

Responsibilities: _____

_____

_____

_____

_____

_____

List 6 major accomplishments (use concrete/quantified dollars, number of products involved, etc., and action words: "reduced, achieved, created, sold, designed, implemented" are grabbing sentence starters.)

1. _____

_____

2. _____

_____

3. _____

_____

4. _____

_____

5. _____

_____

6. _____

_____

Other (promotions, salary increases, transfers, new titles, etc.):

_____

_____

_____

_____

_____

Major decisions, recommendations adopted by company:

_____

_____

_____

_____

_____

_____

_____

_____

Previous employers (follow same format as with more recent

companies): _____

_____

_____

_____

_____

_____

_____

EDUCATION

Degree: _____ Date received: _____

School: _____

Major: _____

Minor: _____

Class rank: _____

Average: _____

Scholarships, prizes, honors: _____

Other degrees, etc. _____

_____

_____

Relevant courses taken: _____

_____

_____

Extra curricular activities: _____

_____

_____

Percent of school expenses earned: _____

At what jobs? _____

_____

_____

_____

Training courses and seminars since school: _____

_____

_____

_____

_____

MILITARY SERVICE

Branch: _____

Specialty: _____

Dates: From: _____ To: _____

Entering rank: _____

Rank at discharge: _____

Training: _____

Relevant responsibilities: _____

_____

_____

_____

_____

_____

_____

Locations of assignments: _____

_____

_____

_____

_____

_____

_____

_____

APPENDIX IV

SAMPLE INTERVIEW QUESTIONS

What jobs have you held? Please explain any time gaps. _____

_____

_____

_____

Earnings at each company? _____

_____

_____

Are you still employed? _____

_____

What are your short-range objectives? _____

_____

_____

_____

What are your long-term objectives? _____

_____

_____

_____

_____

Why are you leaving (or why did you leave) your last com-

pany? _____

_____

Is that the only reason for leaving? _____

_____

Describe the best boss you ever had, and the worst. Give your

reasons why. _____

_____

_____

_____

_____

What skills do you have to offer? _____

_____

_____

What do you look for in an ideal job? _____

_____

_____

Can you reduce costs (or control inventory, or increase sales,

etc.)? Give me some examples. _____

_____

_____

What elements in a job do you enjoy the most? Enjoy the least?

Why? _____

_____

_____

_____

_____

_____

_____

Are you looking for line or for staff work? Why? _____

_____

_____

What are the accomplishments you are most proud of? _____

_____

_____

_____

What is your major strength? Conversely, what is the area you

feel needs more development? _____

_____

_____

_____

How would your last boss describe you? _____

_____

How did your subordinates like you? _____

_____

Do you have experience in firing anyone? What were the cir-

cumstances? _____

_____

_____

_____

How would your spouse describe you? _____

_____

_____

What do you look for when hiring someone? _____

_____

_____

Let's talk now about your education: What was your major?

Why did you choose it? _____

_____

_____

_____

_____

What was your grade point? _____

_____

_____

_____

How did you select a college? _____

_____

_____

Why did you feel you needed a college degree? Why didn't you

go for an advanced degree? _____

_____

_____

_____

What were your favorite subjects? Why? What were your

grades? _____

_____

_____

_____

_____

_____

What was your rank in your graduating class? Could you have

done better? Why didn't you do better? _____

_____

_____

_____

_____

What were your extracurricular activities at school? _____

_____

_____

Did you work during the school year? Doing what? _____

_____

_____

_____

Did you work during the summers? At what kinds of jobs? __

_____

_____

_____

Who paid for your tuition? _____

_____

_____

Do you plan on taking any more courses at night, or going for

an advanced degree? _____

_____

_____

Returning to you, now, what kind of salary are you looking

for? Are you worth it? _____

_____

_____

_____

_____

_____

_____

_____

What job title would you like? How long would you be happy

with that? _____

_____

_____

Would you go after your boss's job? _____

_____

_____

Why do you want a job with our company? _____

_____

_____

_____

If you had a choice, what would be your ideal job and company? Why? _____

_____

_____

Do you have any offers from other companies? _____

_____

How are you different from other candidates for this job? Why should we consider you? _____

_____

_____

_____

_____

_____

_____

_____

Do you have upper-management potential? _____

_____

_____

_____

_____

Do you have any problem with relocating? _____

_____

What percent of your time could you travel on business?

_____

_____

Do you have any limits on working late or overtime? _____

_____

_____

_____

What are your views on motivating people? _____

_____

_____

_____

_____

Do you have a philosophy of management? _____

_____

_____

_____

_____

_____

What books have you read lately? _____

_____

_____

_____

_____

What magazines do you read regularly? Newspapers? _____

_____

_____

_____

_____

What programs do you watch on television? _____

_____

Do you have any hobbies? _____

_____

_____

_____

Do you have any involvement in community affairs? Why?

_____

_____

_____

_____

What size company would you like to work for? Why? _____

_____

_____

_____

What job would you like to have, or will deserve to have, five

years from now? _____

_____

_____

_____

What salary should you be worth in five years? _____

_____

_____

_____

Tell me about yourself—start any place or time period you

want. _____

_____

_____

_____

_____

How is your health? _____

_____

Do you have five business references you can give me? _____

_____

_____

_____

_____

How do you rate yourself as a manager? _____

_____

_____

_____

Why are you still out of work? _____

_____

_____

_____

Tell me about your last boss. _____

_____

_____

_____

Consider your age and experience. Why aren't your earnings

more than they are now? _____

_____

_____

_____

_____

_____

_____

_____

_____

Can you work well with a boss of the opposite sex? _____

_____

_____

_____

If you had it to do over again, what would you change? _____

_____

_____

_____

What personality types seem to bother you the most? _____

_____

_____

_____

_____

Are there any questions you want to ask of me? _____

_____

_____

_____

_____

_____

_____

_____

_____

_____

_____

_____

_____

_____

_____

INDEX